Getting Started with UDOO

Become an efficient maker by designing and building
amazing prototypes with the UDOO platform and
Android

Emanuele Palazzetti

[PACKT] open source *

PUBLISHING

community experience distilled

BIRMINGHAM - MUMBAI

Getting Started with UDOO

First published: February 2015

Production reference: 1170215

Published by Packt Publishing Ltd.
Livery Place
35 Livery Street
Birmingham B3 2PB, UK.

ISBN 978-1-78439-194-2

www.packtpub.com

Credits

Author
Emanuele Palazzetti

Reviewers
Maurizio Caporali

Bill Gatliff

Christian Gil González

Edward Jahn Sayadian

Primiano Tucci

Commissioning Editor
Amit Ghodke

Acquisition Editor
Reshma Raman

Content Development Editor
Ruchita Bhansali

Technical Editor
Abhishek R. Kotian

Copy Editor
Laxmi Subramanian

Project Coordinator
Krani Berde

Proofreaders
Ameesha Green

Stephen Copestake

Cathy Cumberlidge

Indexer
Mariammal Chettiyar

Graphics
Valentina D'silva

Production Coordinator
Melwyn D'sa

Cover Work
Melwyn D'sa

Foreword

This book addresses two very important topics: "Programming" and "Programming with Android".

Programming nowadays is indeed more and more tied to interactions with physical space—you can no longer think about programming only pixels of a screen. Thanks to the evolution of mobile devices, application design and development has encountered a vision change. Today, accelerations and physical rotations of devices are managed by software; information changes depending on the geographic location and on common activities such as walking, driving, travelling, and so on. The next step is programming physical objects connected to the Internet, making our houses, cars, and clothes interactive. This book has the merit to introduce this new vision, showing how simple it is to program real objects, creating new smart ones this way. And it fulfils this goal with an UDOO board, Arduino and Android, starting with a simple Android application that lets you control sensor lights, temperature range, LED lights, and lots more.

UDOO, in fact, allows rapid prototyping of projects based on Arduino: the advantage is a tiny computer that is integrated to the Arduino microcontroller, running Android and Linux. The first few chapters highlight how to realize the connection between Android and Arduino, a very simple task due to the Android Accessory Development Kit (ADK) communication protocol, which is UDOO-compatible. The author, to further simplify the implementation of the protocol, introduces an external library, which allows you, with few lines of code, to connect Android to the real world.

After this first introductory part, you are pushed into the DIY philosophy: start getting your hands dirty, which is the most interesting part. There are several examples and no need for great tools. With just a wooden peg and a light sensor, you can build a heartbeat monitor with the added possibility of visualizing and managing data.

Going forward, in the book, you will see more complex projects, but you will also discover how simple it is to realize the interaction between software and the real world.

This is the fundamental aspect: opening up your imagination and giving new perspectives to software developers.

Maurizio Caporali

Product Manager and Cofounder of UDOO

About the Author

Emanuele Palazzetti is a software developer with strong JavaScript knowledge and a solid background in Python development. Part of his job entails taking care of backend web applications mostly built with the Django web framework. In the past few years, he has delved into many well-known frontend frameworks, such as AngularJS and EmberJS, to strengthen his JavaScript knowledge. Being a former Java developer, he leveraged his previous knowledge and started working on Android; by combining his interest on electronics and embedded devices with the well-known mobile platform, he managed to build several prototypes and small physical applications.

He currently works at Evonove, a small company where he has been leading a number of frontend software projects mostly based on the AngularJS framework. He is also an open source advocate, active contributor, and speaker at Python and Android conferences. He writes about JavaScript and other development stuff at `http://palazzetti.me`.

Many people have helped this book happen. Reshma Raman, Acquisition Editor at Packt Publishing, gave me the opportunity to write this book and Ruchita Bhansali, Content Development Editor at Packt Publishing, provided great support and encouragement during book writing and reviewing. Many thanks to the entire team at Packt Publishing that worked hard and provided suggestions to improve the content of this book.

Thanks to Maurizio Caporali, Primiano Tucci, Edward Sayadian, and Christian Gil González for their valuable and welcomed feedback, which was critical for better clarity and accuracy of the material in this book.

Thanks to Massimiliano Pippi, a colleague and a friend of mine, for his suggestions and feedback during the initial draft.

About the Reviewers

Maurizio Caporali is the CEO and cofounder of AIDILAB s.r.l. (www.aidilab.com) and the cofounder and product manager of UDOO (www.udoo.org).

Maurizio is an information technology expert, services consultant, and service designer for mobile devices applications, and PhD in information and communication technologies. His research interests include physical computing, interaction design, embedded systems, and Internet of Things.

Currently, Maurizio is mainly involved in the UDOO lifecycle management and he is working on different projects regarding the design of new technological products for the home automation, wearable, and cyber physical system market.

Christian Gil González works as a biomedical applications developer and was studying for a degree in computer engineering while this book was being written.

In his current job, he is developing an AllinOne medical point using an UDOO and some medical sensors such as ECG, SpO2, Blood Pressure, and Glucometer.

> I would like to thank my girlfriend for putting up with me during all the time I invested in this book, and to Angela, for helping me to improve my English. I would also like to thank all employees of Imaxdi for giving me the opportunity to work with UDOO and open up the range of possibilities to develop applications for biotechnology.

Edward Jahn Sayadian is a network engineer and teaches network security and network engineering in Sydney, Australia. He has an unquenchable thirst for knowledge, which extends to his hobbies in motor mechanics, electronics, and programming. You can see some of Edward's projects on his blog, `http://www.makeitbreakitfixit.com/`, or find his projects online in the Arduino, UDOO, Kleb, and other hacking communities.

Thanks to my wife, Marlène, for her encouragement and infinite patience and to my son, Ari, for bringing such happiness to our lives that we had never expected or experienced.

You are the water in my watermelon.

Primiano Tucci is a software engineer, hardware enthusiast, extreme DIYer and PhD in real-time embedded systems who enjoys working on open source projects.

www.PacktPub.com

Support files, eBooks, discount offers, and more

For support files and downloads related to your book, please visit www.PacktPub.com.

Did you know that Packt offers eBook versions of every book published, with PDF and ePub files available? You can upgrade to the eBook version at www.PacktPub.com and as a print book customer, you are entitled to a discount on the eBook copy. Get in touch with us at service@packtpub.com for more details.

At www.PacktPub.com, you can also read a collection of free technical articles, sign up for a range of free newsletters and receive exclusive discounts and offers on Packt books and eBooks.

https://www2.packtpub.com/books/subscription/packtlib

Do you need instant solutions to your IT questions? PacktLib is Packt's online digital book library. Here, you can search, access, and read Packt's entire library of books.

Why subscribe?

- Fully searchable across every book published by Packt
- Copy and paste, print, and bookmark content
- On demand and accessible via a web browser

Free access for Packt account holders

If you have an account with Packt at www.PacktPub.com, you can use this to access PacktLib today and view 9 entirely free books. Simply use your login credentials for immediate access.

Table of Contents

Preface

Since the beginning of the 2000s, a global rekindled interest in hardware manufacturing occurred, due to many advances in engineering and microelectronics, which granted the proliferation of new kinds of inexpensive manufacturing tools. People of all ages, even children, started to convert their broken devices, old toys, and every unused piece of hardware, into new amazing objects. This unconventional approach to design and creating something new was characterized by a new way to express creativity, and this was the key factor that created the maker culture.

This was the maker revolution, a movement that changed our world radically. Open source projects provided all the required tools to unleash the creativity to build something, without the need for a strong knowledge in programming and engineering, nor a set of expensive components. Indeed, one of the most important successes achieved by the maker revolution was the capability to move prototypes manufacturing from small or big industries to our homes.

In February 2012, another open source project, called UDOO, started a prototyping board featuring Linux and Android operating systems, with the goal of combining the winning characteristics of Arduino and Raspberry Pi in one single board. After a year working on this project, in April 2013, the UDOO board joined the Kickstarter crowdfunding platform, and the feedback from the maker community was overwhelmingly positive — the project was funded in just 2 days.

Makers all over the world liked the project so much that they decided to contribute, not only through Kickstarter pledges, but even through useful ideas and advice during the board design phase. The result of the help provided by the maker community is a powerful prototyping board to build interactive and creative ideas we always wanted.

This book will teach you how to build your first hardware projects using the UDOO board as a fast prototyping tool. Starting with a simple application that involves the use of basic electronic components, you will work through different projects that let you build electronic circuits, with improved interactions and offered by the Android operating system.

What this book covers

Chapter 1, *Turn On the Engines*, walks you through the setup of the UDOO platform and the required development environment. It begins with an introduction of the board, showing its peculiarity and capabilities that distinguish it from the others; then it guides you through the installation of the Android operating system. The last part, explains how to configure the development environment, both for Arduino and Android, to launch the first Hello World Android application.

Chapter 2, *Know your Tools*, teaches how the Android application is capable of controlling connected devices. It begins with some onboard Arduino characteristics and then explains how to create the first Android application that is capable of communicating with the integrated Arduino device. It then shows how to create a fully functional circuit using a breadboard for fast prototyping.

Chapter 3, *Testing your Physical Application*, explains the main concept behind physical application testing. The first part shows how to build a circuit that is testable from a software application. It then shows how to implement a diagnostic mode to test whether the connected circuit is working correctly.

Chapter 4, *Using Sensors to Listen to the Environment*, begins by explaining how sensors work and how they can be used to make the prototype context aware. It then shows how to build a heartbeat monitor, coding an Arduino sketch to read the sensor's data, and an Android application to visualize the computed results.

Chapter 5, *Managing Interactions with Physical Components*, teaches how to manage user interactions. It starts by explaining some components that can be used to let the outside world interact with the system. It then shows how to build a web radio with a physical controller to manage the prototype volume and to change the current station. In the last part, an Android API is used to playback Internet radio streaming.

Chapter 6, *Building a Chronotherm for Home Automation*, explains how to use some UDOO capabilities for home automation. It shows the creation of a Chronotherm using a circuit to detect environment temperature, and an Android user interface to visualize sensor data and to change the desired temperatures for each time interval.

Chapter 7, Using Android APIs for Human Interaction, adds more functionality to the application from the previous chapter extending the settings management to store different presets using voice recognition and synthesis to manage users' interactions.

Chapter 8, Adding Network Capabilities, extends the Chronotherm application again with the capability to collect forecast data through a RESTful web service. In the last part, it shows how to use collected data to provide more functionalities to the Chronotherm.

Chapter 9, Monitoring your Devices with MQTT, teaches the main concepts of the Internet of Things and the MQTT protocol, used to exchange data between physical devices. It then shows how to set up a cloud-based MQTT broker, capable of receiving and dispatching the Chronotherm temperature updates. The last part shows how to write a standalone Android application to receive the sent data from the Chronotherm.

This a bonus chapter and is downloaded from the following link:
`https://www.packtpub.com/sites/default/files/downloads/1942OS_`
`Chapter_9.pdf`

What you need for this book

In order to run the code demonstrated in this book, you need to configure the development environment, both for Android and Arduino, and a dual or a quad UDOO board with the Android operating system installed, as described in the *Downloading and installing Android* and *Setting up the development environment* section in *Chapter 1, Turn On the Engines.*

Who this book is for

This book is for Android developers who want to apply their skills to build real-world devices capable of interacting with the surrounding environment and to communicate with Android applications. A basic knowledge of Android programming is required to start building real-world devices powered by Android. Prior knowledge of prototyping platforms or circuit building isn't required.

This book will teach you the basics of creating real-world devices through some electronic components that are regularly used during prototype building, and how to integrate them with the Android user interface.

Conventions

In this book, you will find a number of styles of text that distinguish between different kinds of information. Here are some examples of these styles, and an explanation of their meaning.

Code words in text are shown as follows: "The `play()` method sets the streaming URL of the current active station and starts the async prepare."

A block of code is set as follows:

```
public class HelloWorld extends Activity {
  @Override
  protected void onCreate(Bundle savedInstanceState) {
    super.onCreate(savedInstanceState);
    setContentView(R.layout.activity_hello_world);
  }
}
```

When we wish to draw your attention to a particular part of a code block, the relevant lines or items are set in bold:

```
public class HelloWorld extends Activity {
  @Override
  protected void onCreate(Bundle savedInstanceState) {
    super.onCreate(savedInstanceState);
    setContentView(R.layout.activity_hello_world);
  }
}
```

New terms and **important words** are shown in bold. Words that you see on the screen, in menus or dialog boxes for example, appear in the text like this: "For the purpose of this HelloWorld application, select a **Blank Activity** and click **Next**."

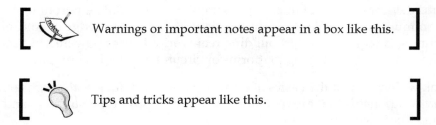

> Warnings or important notes appear in a box like this.

> Tips and tricks appear like this.

Reader feedback

Feedback from our readers is always welcome. Let us know what you think about this book — what you liked or may have disliked. Reader feedback is important for us to develop titles that you really get the most out of.

To send us general feedback, simply send an e-mail to feedback@packtpub.com, and mention the book title via the subject of your message.

If there is a topic that you have expertise in and you are interested in either writing or contributing to a book, see our author guide on www.packtpub.com/authors.

Customer support

Now that you are the proud owner of a Packt book, we have a number of things to help you to get the most from your purchase.

Downloading the example code

You can download the example code files for all Packt books you have purchased from your account at http://www.packtpub.com. If you purchased this book elsewhere, you can visit http://www.packtpub.com/support and register to have the files e-mailed directly to you.

Errata

Although we have taken every care to ensure the accuracy of our content, mistakes do happen. If you find a mistake in one of our books — maybe a mistake in the text or the code — we would be grateful if you would report this to us. By doing so, you can save other readers from frustration and help us improve subsequent versions of this book. If you find any errata, please report them by visiting http://www.packtpub.com/submit-errata, selecting your book, clicking on the **errata submission form** link, and entering the details of your errata. Once your errata are verified, your submission will be accepted and the errata will be uploaded on our website, or added to any list of existing errata, under the Errata section of that title. Any existing errata can be viewed by selecting your title from http://www.packtpub.com/support.

Piracy

Piracy of copyright material on the Internet is an ongoing problem across all media. At Packt, we take the protection of our copyright and licenses very seriously. If you come across any illegal copies of our works, in any form, on the Internet, please provide us with the location address or website name immediately so that we can pursue a remedy.

Please contact us at copyright@packtpub.com with a link to the suspected pirated material.

We appreciate your help in protecting our authors, and our ability to bring you valuable content.

Questions

You can contact us at questions@packtpub.com if you are having a problem with any aspect of the book, and we will do our best to address it.

1
Turn On the Engines

Any idea should start with a prototype. It doesn't matter whether it's a game, a web or mobile application, or a generic software component. Every time we want to deliver something to our final users, we have to create a prototype first. This is the most important step because it's when we start to face our first difficulties and when we may change some important aspects of our project.

If we are writing a software component, the first prototype isn't too expensive because what we need is our time and passion. However, this isn't applicable when our project has some hardware parts because it could be too expensive to afford all the required components. This statement was true until programmers, engineers and open source lovers started to release projects such as **Arduino**.

Fast prototyping boards let people realize projects with cheap or reused old components, and this, together with the **Do It Yourself** (**DIY**) philosophy, allows the creation of a huge community that spreads all over the world. This is where the UDOO board plays an important role in the makers' community: the hardware prototyping ecosystem, together with the traditional way to write software applications, represents a powerful combination for interactive projects creation.

In this chapter, we will explore more details about the UDOO board, focusing on the elements that are important to get started. In particular, we will cover:

- Exploring the UDOO platform and its main characteristics
- Setting up the board with the Android operating system
- Configuring the development environment for Arduino and Android
- Bootstrapping a simple Android application
- Deploying an Android application

Introducing the UDOO platform

The UDOO board is designed to offer us great flexibility with the tools, the programming language, and the environment in which we build the first prototype. The main goal of the board is to take part in the era of the *Internet of Things* and this is why an embedded Atmel SAM3X8E ARM Cortex-M3 processor is its first building block.

This processor is the same that powers the Arduino Due board and it's fully compliant to Arduino pinout. The result of this feature is that the board is compatible with all Arduino Due shields and most of Arduino Uno shields, so developers can convert and reuse their old programs and circuits.

 The UDOO I/O pins are 3.3V compliant. For instance, if you're using a sensor powered by 5V that outputs the signal to UDOO pins at 3.3V, then you're fine. On the other hand, if the sensor outputs the signal to UDOO at 5V, it will damage your board. Every time you're using a shield or a sensor, be aware of provided output voltage to UDOO pins. This precaution is the same for a traditional Arduino Due board.

The second building block is a powerful Freescale i.MX 6 ARM Cortex-A9 processor, which is shipped in Dual and Quad core versions. The official supported operating system is *UDOObuntu*, which is a *Lubuntu 12.04 LTS armHF* based operating system that ships out of the box with many pre-installed tools to be up and running quickly. Indeed, after your first boot, you have a fully configured development environment to program the onboard Arduino from the board itself.

Despite that, what makes UDOO really different from other boards is the **Android support**. With the capability to run smoothly, this operating system is a great opportunity for novice or experienced Android developers because they can create a new kind of real-world application that is powered by the Android user interface, its powerful design patterns, and even by other developers' applications.

 Developers can choose to write their real-word applications using the Linux operating system. In this case, they can write web services or desktop applications using many well-known programming languages such as Python, Javascript (Node.js), Php, and Java. However, we will focus on application development under Android.

The latest building block is related to all I/O components. UDOO could be purchased with an internal Wi-Fi and a Gigabit Ethernet, which are recognized by both Linux and Android. It also offers **HDMI (High-Definition Multimedia Interface)** output connection and is shipped with an integrated **Transistor-Transistor Logic (TTL)** to **Low-Voltage Differential Signaling (LVDS)** expansion slot so that developers can connect an external LVDS touch screen.

> During the course of this book, it is assumed that you're connecting UDOO to an external monitor through the HDMI cable. However, if you own an external LVDS panel, you can proceed with the connection just before the *Our first run* section in this chapter. To let Android use the external panel, you should follow some steps that you can find in the official documentation at http://www.udoo.org/faq-items/how-do-i-set-up-my-lvds/.

Another great component that is officially supported is the camera module that is easy to plug in the board and can be used for projects that require computer vision or image analysis. The last integrated component is the audio card with a fully functional audio playback and recording through an external microphone.

The mix of these building blocks, together with the Internet access and many Android APIs, gives us the opportunity to build real-world applications that listen to the environment and talk to devices with a board that can take part in the *Internet of Things*.

Downloading and installing Android

We have an idea about a list of UDOO components that we may use to start building amazing projects. However, before we continue, we need to configure our board to run the Android operating system and also our development environment so that we can start writing and deploying our first application.

> All prototypes you build in this book are based on Android KitKat 4.4.2 that is the latest supported version at the time of this writing. During the course of this book you will build many projects that make use of the **Android Support Library** to ensure compatibility with newer Android versions that the UDOO board will support.

The UDOO board doesn't have internal storage or a built-in boot program because it relies on external storage, a microSD card, in which you can install a bootloader and a compatible operating system. The easiest way to create a bootable microSD card, is to download and copy a precompiled image, though it's possible to create a clean operating system using released binaries and kernel sources.

`http://www.udoo.org/downloads/` points to the official UDOO download page that contains the links for all the available precompiled images.

Among Linux images, we can find and download the latest supported version of Android KitKat 4.4.2. As stated earlier, UDOO comes in two different versions with dual and quad processors so we must download the right version, according to the owned platform.

Installing from Windows

To install the Android image from Windows, you need some extra tools to unpack and copy the image into the microSD card. The downloaded `.zip` file is in 7-Zip compression format, so you need to install a third-party unarchive program such as 7-Zip. When the extracting process is done, we have an uncompressed `.img` file ready for copy on an empty card.

To write the uncompressed image into our microSD card, perform the following steps:

1. Insert your microSD card in the built-in slot reader or external card reader.

2. Format the card using the `FAT32` filesystem.

3. To write the image on the micsoSD card, we need to use the Win32DiskImager tool. Download it from `http://sourceforge.net/projects/win32diskimager/`.

4. Run the application, but bear in mind that if we are using Windows 7 or Window 8.x, we have to right-click on `Win32DiskImager.exe` executable and be sure to select the **Run as administrator** option from the context menu.

5. Win32DiskImager is a tool that writes raw disk images using low-level instructions. This means that you need to exactly follow the next steps and be really sure that you correctly select the output device. If this option is wrong, you might lose all your data from an unwanted storage memory.

6. Once the application starts, you can see the main window, as illustrated in the following screenshot:

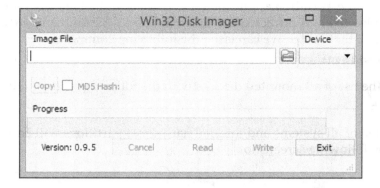

7. From the application's main window, in the **Image File** box, choose the `.img` file previously extracted.

8. Select the microSD drive accurately on the **Device** dropdown and bear in mind that if we use the wrong drive, we can destroy all our data on the computer's hard disk.

9. Click on the **Write** button and wait for the process to complete in order to have a bootable Android operating system in the microSD card.

Installing from Mac OS X

To install the Android image from Mac OS X, we need a third-party tool to unpack the downloaded `.zip` file, because it's in 7-Zip compression format and we can't use the built-in unarchive software. We have to download software such as Keka, which is freely available at `http://www.kekaosx.com/`.

If we love the Mac OS X terminal, we can use the Homebrew package manager that is available at `http://brew.sh/`.

In this case, from the command line, we can simply install the `p7zip` package and use the `7za` utility to unpack the file as follows:

```
brew install p7zip
7za x [path_to_zip_file]
```

To proceed and write the uncompressed image into our microSD card, perform the following steps:

1. Launch the **Terminal** application and enter into the folder in which we have downloaded and extracted the Android image. Assuming `Downloads` is the name of that folder, we can issue the following command:

   ```
   cd Downloads
   ```

2. Get the list of all mounted devices with the following command:

   ```
   df -h
   ```

3. The list of all systems and internal hard drive partitions will be similar to the following screenshot:

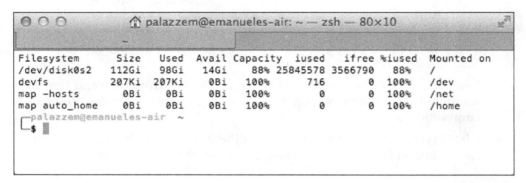

4. Connect the microSD card using the built-in or external card reader.

5. Format the microSD card through the Disk Utility application that is already available in our system. Launch it and select the correct disk from the list on the left.

6. From the main panel of the window, choose the **Erase** tab from the upper menu and select the **MS-DOS (FAT)** filesystem in the **Format** dropdown. When you are ready, click on the **Erase** button.

7. From the Terminal application, launch the previous command again:

   ```
   df -h
   ```

8. The list of mounted partitions has been changed, as we see in the following screenshot:

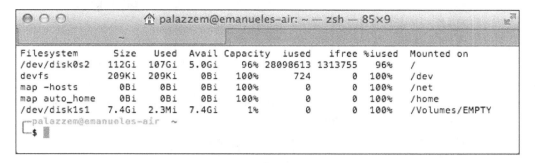

```
Filesystem       Size   Used  Avail Capacity  iused    ifree %iused  Mounted on
/dev/disk0s2     112Gi  107Gi 5.0Gi    96% 28098613 1313755   96%  /
devfs            209Ki  209Ki   0Bi   100%      724       0  100%  /dev
map -hosts         0Bi    0Bi   0Bi   100%        0       0  100%  /net
map auto_home      0Bi    0Bi   0Bi   100%        0       0  100%  /home
/dev/disk1s1     7.4Gi  2.3Mi 7.4Gi     1%        0       0  100%  /Volumes/EMPTY
palazzem@emanueles-air  ~
$
```

9. We can assume that the missing device, during the first run, is our microSD card, so we have to bear in mind the new value under the **Filesystem** column. If you look at the previous screenshot, our partition name is /dev/disk1s1 while it isn't /dev/disk0s2 because it's our hard disk.

10. Once we have found the correct partition, we have to unmount it using the following command:

    ```
    sudo diskutil unmount /dev/[partition_name]
    ```

11. To write the image into the microSD card, we must find the raw disk device so that we can erase and write the Android image into the card. Assuming that the partition name found before was /dev/disk1s1, the related raw disk will be /dev/rdisk1.

> We are going to use the dd tool. This command writes raw disk images using low-level instructions. This means that you need to exactly follow the next steps and be really sure that you choose the correct disk device, because if it is wrong, you can lose all your data from an unwanted storage.

12. Write the image previously extracted into the microSD card using dd with the following command:

    ```
    sudo dd bs=1m if=[udoo_image_name].img of=/dev/[raw_disk_name]
    ```

    A full example of the previous command is as follows:

    ```
    sudo dd bs=1m if=[udoo_image_name].img of=/dev/rdisk1
    ```

13. When we launch the command nothing seems to happen, but actually, dd is writing the Android image in the background. Once the process is complete, it outputs the transferred bytes report, as shown in the following example:

```
6771+1 records in
6771+1 records out
7100656640 bytes transferred in 1395.441422 secs (5088466 bytes/
sec)
```

14. Now we have our bootable Android operating system and we can eject the microSD card with the following command:

```
sudo diskutil eject /dev/[raw_disk_name]
```

Installing from Linux

To install the Android image from Linux, we need a third-party tool to unpack the downloaded .zip file. Because the file is in 7-Zip compression format, we need to install the p7zip package porting from the command line using the package manager of our distribution. Then we can use the 7za utility to unpack the file or any other graphical unarchiver that makes you comfortable.

We can proceed to write the uncompressed image into our microSD card using the following steps:

1. Open the Linux Terminal and enter into the folder where we have downloaded and extracted the Android image. Assuming the file is in our Downloads folder, we can issue the following command:

```
cd Downloads
```

2. Attach the microSD card using the built-in or external card reader.

3. Find the correct device name through the following command:

```
sudo fdisk -l | grep Disk
```

4. The output is a filtered list of all the devices found, and it contains, among others output lines, something like:

```
Disk /dev/sda: 160.0 GB, 160041885696 bytes
Disk /dev/mapper/ubuntu--vg-root: 157.5 GB, 157454172160 bytes
Disk /dev/sdb: 7948 MB, 7948206080 bytes
```

In this case, /dev/sda is our hard disk while /dev/sdb is our microSD card. If this is not your case and you are using an internal card reader, it's possible that the device is named /dev/mmcblk0.

When you've found the right device name, keep it in mind so that we can use it later.

5. Find all the mounted partitions of the above device through the following command:

```
mount | grep [device_name]
```

6. If the previous command generates an output, find the partition name available in the first column of the output and unmount any listed partitions through the following command:

```
sudo umount /dev/[partition_name]
```

 dd is a tool that writes raw disk images using low-level instructions. This means that you need to exactly follow the next steps and be really sure that you choose the correct disk device because, if it is wrong, you can lose all your data from an unwanted storage memory.

7. Write the image previously extracted to the above device name using the dd command:

```
sudo dd bs=1M if=[udoo_image_name].img of=/dev/[device_name]
```

Assuming /dev/sdb is our microSD card, the following is a full example:

```
sudo dd bs=1M if=[udoo_image_name].img of=/dev/sdb
```

8. When we launch the command nothing seems to happen, but actually, dd is writing the image in the background. Once the process is complete, it outputs the transferred bytes report, as follows:

```
6771+1 records in
```

```
6771+1 records out
```

```
7100656640 bytes transferred in 1395.441422 secs (5088466 bytes/sec)
```

9. Now we have our bootable Android operating system and we can eject the microSD card with the following command:

```
sudo eject /dev/[device_name]
```

Our first run

Once we have a bootable microSD card, we can insert it into our UDOO board, use our external monitor or LVDS panel and connect a mouse and a keyboard. After the power is switched on, the Android logo shows up and when the loading process is finished, we can finally see the Android home interface.

Setting up the development environment

Now that Android in our UDOO board is fully functional, it's time to configure the development environment. Every project we're going to build is composed of two different running applications: the first is the physical application composed of an Arduino program capable of controlling an external circuit through UDOO I/O pins; the second one, is an Android application that will run on the board and that deals with the user interface.

Because we have to write two different applications that interact with each other, we need to configure our development environment with two different IDEs.

Installing and using Arduino IDE

Before we can start to upload our programs, we need to install the *microUSB serial port driver* so that we can correctly communicate with onboard Arduino. The USB to the **Universal Asynchronous Receiver/Transmitter (UART)** driver, compatible with the CP210x converter available on the board, can be downloaded from

`http://www.silabs.com/products/mcu/pages/usbtouartbridgevcpdrivers.aspx`.

Here we have to choose the correct version according to our operating system. Once the download is complete, we can extract the archive and double-click on the executable to proceed with the installation. When the installation process is complete, we may need to restart the system.

Now that the microUSB bridge driver is working, from the Arduino website, we have to download the IDE 1.5x beta because, at the moment, the beta version is the only one that supports Arduino Due boards. The link `http://arduino.cc/en/Main/Software#toc3` points directly to the latest version.

To upload a new program, UDOO needs to receive the signals ERASE and RESET from the serial port before and after the upload, respectively. On the official Arduino Due board, this action is performed by the integrated ATmega16U2 microcontroller, which is missing in the UDOO board. The Arduino IDE will take care of this process, but if in the future you prefer to use another IDE, you will have to take care on your own.

Installing in Windows

To install in Windows, we have two different options: use the provided installer or use the archive file for nonadministrator installation. If we choose to use the installer, we can double-click on the executable. When the installer asks us which components we want to install, be sure to select all the checkboxes. If we choose to use the archive file instead of the installer, extract the file and put the result directory into your users folder.

Installing in Mac OS X

To install in Mac OS X, we need to download the archive version. If we run an OS X version greater than 10.7, we can download the Java 7 version. In any other cases, or if you are not sure, download the Java 6 version.

When we finish the download, we have to double-click on the archive to proceed with the extraction and then drag-and-drop the Arduino application icon inside our Applications folder.

Installing in Linux

To install in Linux, we need to download the archive version supported by our 32 or 64 bit architecture. Once the download has finished, we can extract the IDE and put it inside our home folder or in any other folder of your choice.

First launch

Now that we have finished configuring the communication driver and the IDE with the correct patch, we can launch and see the Arduino IDE, as shown in the following screenshot:

Installing and using Android Studio

UDOO with an Android operating system acts like any other traditional Android device. This means we can use the standard toolchain, build system, and IDE used for the development of smartphones or tablets applications. At the moment, the available toolchains are related to two main IDEs: Eclipse and Android Studio.

Eclipse is an open source IDE with an advanced plugin system that allows you to easily extend many of its core capabilities. This brought Google to develop an **Android Development Tool (ADT)** plugin to create an integrated development environment in which developers can write, debug, and package their Android applications.

Android Studio is a more recent project whose first beta was released in May 2013 while the first stable release was in December 2014. Based on IntelliJ IDEA, a well-known Java IDE, it's powered by the **Gradle** build system that combines the flexibility of **Ant** with the dependency management of **Maven**. All these characteristics, together with the increasing number of plugins, best practices, **Google Cloud Platform** integration, and third-party services integration such as **Travis CI**, make Android Studio a great choice for the development of future projects.

All Android projects covered in this book are built using Android Studio, and if you are a novice or an experienced Android developer and Eclipse is your usual IDE, this could be a great opportunity to try the new Android Studio.

The first thing to do is to download the latest version of Android Studio for your operating system from `https://developer.android.com/sdk/`.

When the download starts, we'll be redirected to the installation instructions related to our operating system, and when we finish the installation, we can start the IDE. During the first run, the IDE will make all the required checks to retrieve and install the latest available SDK, virtual device, and build system to let you start developing the first application. In the **Setup Wizard - SDK Settings** page, be sure to select the **Android SDK** and **Android Virtual Device** components and then click on **Next**. In the next page, you should accept all Android licenses and then click on **Finish**.

Once the IDE is installed, we can start Android Studio. The following screenshot shows the main window when a project is not opened:

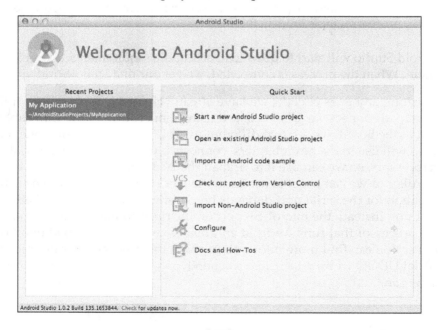

Running your first Android application

Now that Android is installed in our UDOO board and that all development environments are configured, we can start to write and deploy our first Android application. The following is the default pattern of other developers when they start to dive into a new technology. We are going to write and deploy a simple Android application that prints Hello World!.

To bootstrap our first project, perform the following steps:

1. In the main window of Android Studio, click on **Start a new Android Studio project**.

2. In the **Application name** field, type HelloWorld; in **Company domain**, write your domain or example.com if you don't have any at the moment. Then, click on **Next**.

3. In the form factors selection window, select **Phone and Tablet** and choose **API 19: Android 4.4 (KitKat)** in the **Minimum SDK**. Then, click on **Next**.

4. In the add activity page, for the purpose of this hello world application, select a **Blank Activity** option and click on **Next**.

5. In the **Activity Options** page, write *HelloWorld* in **Activity Name** and click on **Finish**.

In next chapters, we will create applications from scratch, so we have to bear in mind the previous steps because we are going to repeat the process multiple times in this book.

Now Android Studio will start to download all Gradle requirements to prepare our build system. When the process is completed, we get our first HelloWorld application.

Without writing any lines of code, we have already created a deployable application. Now we have to connect our UDOO board using a microUSB to the USB cable. If we take a look at the board, we see two different microUSB ports. The first one on the left, that we will use in the next chapters, connects our computer to the serial port of both processors, so we can use it to upload the Arduino program to the UDOO microcontroller or we can use it to access to the Android system shell. The activated communication for the serial port depends on the state of J18 jumper, whether it's plugged or not. Instead, the microUSB port on the right connects our computer to the i.MX 6 processor that runs Android and that we will use to upload our Android applications. You can find more information about the processor communication at the official UDOO website http://www.udoo.org/features/processors-communication/.

To connect our computer to the Android operating system for the application upload process, we need to use the right microUSB port colored in black in the following screenshot:

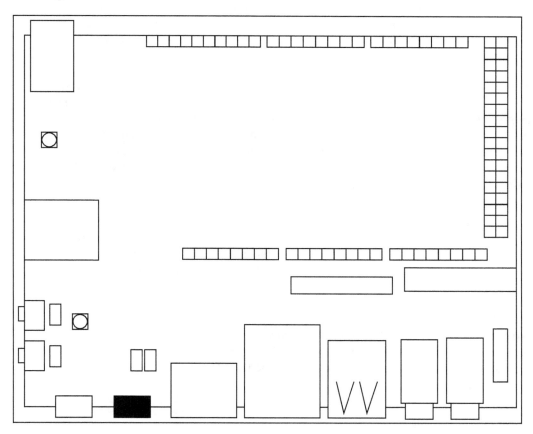

Like we do in a traditional Android application, we can click from the top menu on **Run** and then on **Run app**. At this point, we need to choose a running device, but unfortunately, our list of available devices is empty. This problem occurs because of how the internal communication between processors works.

After the boot time, the connection is enabled between the two processors and plugging the microUSB cable will produce no effect. This happens because Android doesn't use the internal UART serial port during the communication with Arduino. It uses the **USB On-The-Go (OTG)** bus that allows devices to act as host and let other components such as flash drive, mouse, keyboard, or Arduino, in this case, to connect through it.

The i.MX 6 processor is physically connected to the OTG bus while the other side of the bus is connected both to Arduino and to the external microUSB connector. The current active connection can be changed using a software piloted switch. When the external OTG port is enabled, Android can communicate with an external computer via microUSB port but it can't send back any data to onboard Arduino. On the contrary, when the external OTG port is disabled, Android can communicate with Arduino but the connection with the computer is interrupted.

The latter is our actual configuration and we need to switch the OTG port in order to enable the external communication with our computer to complete the application deployment. From Android, we have to go to the **Settings menu** and choose **Developer options**. There we need to select the **External OTG port enabled** checkbox. If the USB cable is connected, a popup will ask us to allow USB debugging. If this is our main computer, we may want to select **Always allow from this computer** and then click on **OK**. If this option is not checked, the popup will be shown every time we connect UDOO to our computer.

Bear in mind that every time we need to deploy our Android application, we need to enable the external OTG port. On the contrary, when our application is deployed and we need Android to communicate with Arduino, we need to disable the external OTG port.

Now that our computer can see the UDOO board as a traditional Android device, we can try to deploy our application again. This time, in the **Choose Device** dialog, we can find a Freescale UDOO Android device. Select it and click on **OK**. Our first deployment is complete and now we can see the HelloWorld application on the connected monitor.

Summary

In this chapter, we learned some UDOO characteristics that distinguish this board from the others. One of the greatest differences is related to the full support of the Android platform that led us to install and configure the latest supported version on the board.

We explored the necessary tools to start developing real-world applications and we configured our development environment to write Android applications and Arduino programs.

We had a brief introduction about how the communication between the two processors works and how we can switch the OTG port to enable external access for our first deployment. In the next chapter, we will start a new Android application from scratch that is capable of using and controlling a physical device built through a set of prototyping tools.

2
Know Your Tools

As discussed in the last chapter, real-world applications aren't just software. They are composed of simple or complex circuits that perform actions in the physical world. Before we start to build our first interactive project, we need to know how these physical components work, so that we know what's inside our toolbox.

In this chapter, we will cover the following topics:

- Uploading the first Arduino program
- Enabling a connection with Arduino
- Writing an Android application capable of acting as a controller
- Building a simple circuit controlled by Android

Introducing Arduino Due capabilities

The physical world is composed of many forms of energy that we perceive in the form of light, heat, sound, or motion. While driving a car when we are near traffic lights and see a red light up ahead, we start to slow down and stop the car. We are just sensing a light form of energy and this led us to change our activity because someone taught us what every traffic light's phase means.

This natural behavior is the same we want to bring to our interactive physical applications. We use hardware devices called **sensors** that listen to the environment and that cooperate with other hardware components, called **actuators**, which perform actions in the real world. However, we need a third element called **microcontroller** that uses connected sensors and actuators to sense and alter the surrounding environment, according to the uploaded program.

The onboard Arduino Due bears the latest part and provides a common way to connect external electronic components. It has 54 digital I/O pins that we can use to send or receive digital signals. This is particularly useful when we want to gather inputs from external devices such as switches or push buttons, while we can send digital signals to turn simple components on or off. In the following diagram, you can see all the digital pins in black:

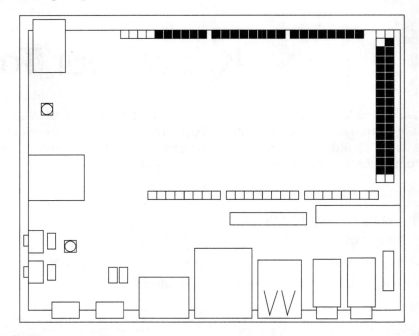

We have 12 analog inputs at our disposal, with a 12 bits resolution for 4096 different values for reading. They are useful when we need to collect data from our sensors and use the returned value as a condition for our program to change the behavior of our physical device. Good examples of read values are related to temperature, light, or proximity sensors. The board also offers 2 **Digital to Analog Converters (DAC)**, with a 12 bits resolution, which can be used as analog output when we have to use a digital signal to drive an analog device. A good example of when you've to use DAC I/O pins is when you have to create an audio output with your device. In the following diagram, you will find all analog pins marked in black, while the 2 DAC pins are marked in gray:

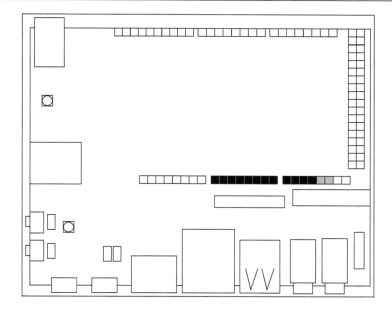

With these functionalities, we have all the required tools to control little devices from our Android applications. On the other hand, we can also take advantages from the inverse and let connected devices change the behavior of our Android interface.

However, UDOO becomes really powerful when used to pilot a complex circuit that may need a hardware driver to interact with it. This could become the usual approach when we are going to recycle devices that we already own, such as old toys, or when we are buying new things such as little motorized robots or rovers.

Building hardware drivers is an expensive task that requires a lot of experience in software and electronics. UDOO, through the onboard Arduino, makes this task easy because it reuses all components built from the makers community. We can add other functionalities combining UDOO with a *shield*, which is a pluggable board that implements a complex circuit with all the required hardware logic. Good examples are LCD Arduino compatible screens, Bluetooth controllers and motor shields to control connected motors, with a few lines of code and without the need to build an external circuit.

Uploading the first program

Now that we know what are the main components and capabilities of our UDOO board, we can start to write and upload our first program. We have to keep in mind that, even if the SAM3X is a standalone processor, we need a working microSD card with a valid UDOO image, otherwise the Arduino programmer will not work.

As we did earlier for Android, we are going to write a simple application that prints Hello World! on our screen, without any Android interaction at the moment. Before opening the Arduino IDE, we need to connect the board to our computer via the microUSB port, available on the left of the board, as you can see in the following schema:

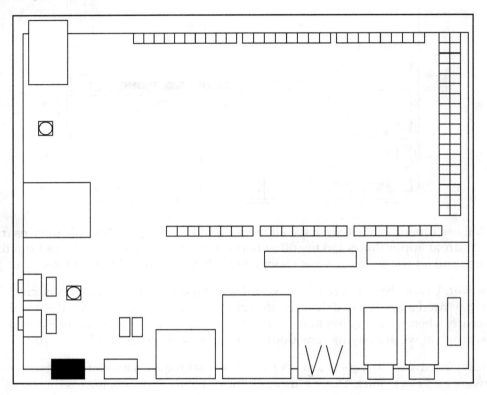

However, this connection isn't enough to allow a correct communication between the Arduino SAM3X and our computer because both the processors use this microUSB port to communicate via a serial port with the connected device. An internal physical switch chooses the connected processor between the i.MX6 that runs Android and the Arduino SAM3X.

This is a different connection and not the same used in the previous chapter. It refers to the serial port and must not be confused with the OTG microUSB port used for the deployment of Android applications.

To enable the connection between our computer and the SAM3X, we must unplug the physical **jumper J18** as we can see in the following schema:

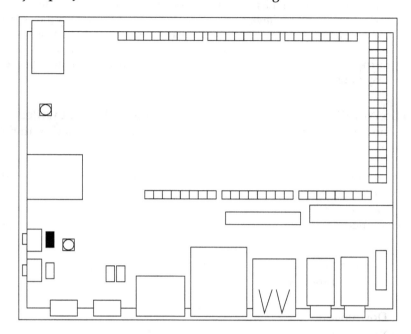

Now we are ready to launch the Arduino IDE and proceed to write and upload our first program. When the IDE shows up, it will open an empty program. Every program and code written for Arduino is called a **sketch**. Arduino sketches are written using a simplified set of C/C++, and if you are interested, you can find a full reference at `http://arduino.cc/en/Reference/HomePage`.

The initial sketch contains two functions as follows:

- `setup()`: This is called once during the initial execution and there we put all initial configurations
- `loop()`: This is called over and over until someone turns off the device, and it represents the core of our sketch

All our sketches must contain both functions, otherwise our program will not work. We may add our own functions to make the code more readable and reusable, so we can embrace the programming principle **Don't Repeat Yourself (DRY)**.

We must bear in mind that we are going to write software for a microcontroller that has at most 512 KB of available memory to store the code. Moreover, we have the 96 KB of SRAM limit in which the sketch creates and manipulates variables at runtime. For complex projects, we should always optimize our code to reduce the used memory, but for the purpose of this book, we write the code so that it's more readable and easy to implement.

To print Hello World! on our screen, we need to code a sketch that writes a String into the built-in serial port. This sketch can be implemented with the following easy steps:

1. In the `setup()` function, initialize the serial port with the specified data rate expressed in **bits per second (baud)**, as follows:

    ```
    void setup() {
      Serial.begin(115200);
    }
    ```

    We choose `115200` baud per second, because the onboard Arduino Due supports this data rate.

Downloading the example code

You can download the example code files for all Packt books you have purchased from your account at http://www.packtpub.com. If you purchased this book elsewhere, you can visit http://www.packtpub.com/support and register to have the files e-mailed directly to you.

2. Write into the serial port using the `println()` function within the main `loop()` function:

    ```
    void loop() {
      Serial.println("Hello World!");
    }
    ```

    Even if we are tempted to upload our project, we have to bear in mind that the `loop()` function is called over and over and this means that maybe we will receive too many Hello World! instances. A good thing is to add a `delay()` function so that Arduino waits for the given milliseconds before starting with the `loop()` function again.

3. To print one sentence per second, add the highlighted code as follows:

    ```
    void loop() {
      Serial.println("Hello World!");
      delay(1000);
    }
    ```

Now we are ready to start the upload process. It consists of two phases where our code is first compiled and then uploaded to the SAM3X processor. If we upload two different sketches, the latest one overrides the first one because we can load and execute only one sketch at a time.

In this case, we need to configure the IDE so it can program the correct board connected to the correct serial port. Click on **Tools**, hover over **Boards** and choose **Arduino Due (programming port)**. Now click on **Tools**, hover over **Port**, and choose your configured port. The correct port depends on your operating system and usually they have the following values:

- In Windows: The COM port with the highest number
- In Mac OS X: /dev/tty.SLAB_USBtoUART
- In Linux: /dev/ttyUSB0

To upload the program, click on **File** and then on **Upload** or use the shortcut available in the toolbar. If the upload process goes fine, you will see the logger with the following output in the bottom of the window:

To be sure that our first sketch works as expected, we need to use a serial port reader, and the Arduino IDE provides a built-in serial monitor. Click on **Tools** and then on **Serial Monitor**, or use the shortcut available in the toolbar. We may see some strange characters and this occurs because the serial monitor is configured by default to read the serial at 9600 baud. In the bottom-right dropdown, select **115200 baud** to see the following output:

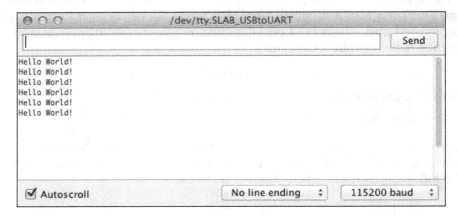

 Using the `Serial.println()` function allows you to send data through the serial port. This is not used to communicate with the i.MX6 processor, but it's a great way to debug variables or your sketch flow from your computer.

When we've finished the sketch upload, we can plug in the **J18 jumper**. Now that we know how to deploy Android applications and Arduino sketches, it's time to start from scratch and build our first project.

Interacting with the real world

Our first real-world prototype should be an Android application that we can use to control a simple electronic component. We have to choose something that is not too trivial, so we can experiment with it, but also that it is not too complex, so we can dive into all main concepts without too many implementation details. A good starting point is the creation of a controller that we can use to turn on and off a real **Light Emitting Diode (LED)** component.

However, before we proceed, we have to understand how to create a communication between the Android application and the sketch. During the deployment process, we used to enable the external OTG port to communicate with the i.MX6 processor from our computer. If we disable this option, an internal switch activates a bidirectional communication between the i.MX6 and the SAM3X processors. This is possible because Arduino Due has full support for USB OTG connection and we are using this connection to let Android and Arduino communicate with each other.

Unfortunately, the above software switch isn't very useful if we don't have a communication protocol. This is where the **Accessory Development Kit (ADK)** plays an important role. It's a reference implementation developed by Google to build Android accessories and it provides a set of software libraries. UDOO board has the full support of ADK. By combining the internal Android APIs with the external Arduino library, we can easily use this functionality to send commands and receive data. In this way, our Android sees our Arduino device like an *Android accessory* so that the connection is supported in our application and in the whole system. We can find further details about ADK at `http://developer.android.com/tools/adk/index.html`.

Communicating with Arduino

The first step of this prototype is to start a new sketch and set up the initial connection from the Arduino side. On the top of our empty sketch, we should add the following code:

```
#include <adk.h>
#define BUFFSIZE 128
#define LED 2
```

The `adk.h` header file contains all the required declarations for many utilities and functions that we can use, for example, to initialize the ADK connection, to send hardware information to Android, and read and write buffered data between the two processors. In the preceding code, we're also defining two *macro objects*, which, respectively, provide the maximum dimension of the read and write buffer and what is the used pinout to turn on and off the LED. We have to keep in mind this number because we will reuse it later when we connect our first electronic component.

Through the protocol used by the ADK, Arduino is recognized by Android like an external accessory. To distinguish our accessory among the others, Android needs an **accessory descriptor** that we can provide with the following code:

```
char accessoryName[] = "LED lamp";
char manufacturer[] = "Example, Inc.";
```

```
char model[] = "LedLamp";
char versionNumber[] = "0.1.0";
char serialNumber[] = "1";
char url[] = "http://www.example.com";
```

Here, we provide information about the accessory name, the name of the hardware manufacturer and the unique identifier of the model. Other than these prototype descriptors, we have to define the hardware version and the serial number because they are strongly required when we connect the device to the Android application. Indeed, the versionNumber, the model and the manufacturer parameters will be matched with the values we provide to the Android application later, and if there is a mismatch, our sketch will not be recognized by the Android application. In this way, we can also maintain a strong binding between the application version and the hardware version in order to avoid an older Android application wrongly controlling a new hardware release.

> The preceding descriptor is required to recognize the sketch and the hardware from the Android application. However, bear in mind that this is a part of good *programming etiquette* and that, for every application and prototype, you should always provide version numbering together with a change log. In this book, we will use **semantic versioning** and you can find more information about it at http://semver.org.

The latest parameter is the url that is used by Android to redirect users to a website where they can find further information about the connected accessory. Android will show that message every time it does not find an installed application capable of managing the interaction with the Arduino accessory.

> In most cases, it's a good idea to set the url parameter with a link that will download and install the packaged Android application. In this way, if the Android application is missing, we are providing a fast way to retrieve and install it, and this is particularly useful when we're distributing schematics and sketches of our prototypes to other developers. You can find further information about how to create a packaged application with Android Studio at https://developer.android.com/tools/building/building-studio.html.

To finish the ADK configuration, we have to add the following code below the previous declarations:

```
uint8_t buffer[BUFFSIZE];
uint32_t bytesRead = 0;
USBHost Usb;
```

```
ADK adk(&Usb, manufacturer, model, accessoryName, versionNumber, url,
serialNumber);
```

We are declaring the used `buffer` parameter during read and write operations and an `USBHost` object. We use it to initialize the connection in the main `loop()` function so that Android receives all the required information during the discovery process. In the last line, we are initializing the ADK accessory descriptor with defined values.

To start the connection, we should put the following code into the `loop()` function:

```
void loop(){
  Usb.Task();
  if (adk.isReady()) {
   // Do something
  }
}
```

The `Usb.Task()` function call polls connected USB devices for updates to their status and waits for 5 seconds to see whether any devices respond to the update request. When Android responds to the polling, we use a conditional statement to evaluate the `adk.isReady()` function call. It returns `True` when the device is connected and ready to communicate with Android, so we know exactly when the Android system reads the prototype descriptor and when it notifies the installed applications that a new accessory is connected.

Our initial configuration is done and we can upload our sketch into the board. When the sketch is uploaded and we disable the OTG external port, Android will discover the running accessory and then show a message to notify users that there aren't any available applications that will work with the attached USB accessory. It also gives users the opportunity to follow the chosen URL, as you can see in the following screenshot:

LED lamp

No installed apps work with this USB accessory. Learn more about this accessory at http://www.example.com

Cancel   View

Writing an Android application controller

Our first building block is ready, but at the moment it doesn't have any physical actuator that we can use, nor a user interface to control it. For this reason, our next step is to create our second Android project through Android Studio called **LEDLamp**. As we did in our first application, remember to choose **API level 19** and a **Blank Activity** that we can call **LightSwitch**.

When the activity editor shows up, it would be a good idea to change the visual preview of the user interface because we're going to use the monitor view instead of a common smartphone view. We can change it through the **Preview** tab that you can find on the right of the application screen and there we can select **Android TV (720p)**from the contextual menu.

Because we need a really simple activity, we have to change the default layout using the following steps:

1. In the `res/layout/activity_light_switch.xml` file, change the `RelativeLayout` parameter in a vertical `LinearLayout` parameter, as you can see in the following code that is highlighted:

    ```
    <LinearLayout
    xmlns:android="http://schemas.android.com/apk/res
    /android"
     xmlns:tools="http://schemas.android.com/tools"
     android:orientation="vertical"
     android:layout_width="match_parent"
     android:layout_height="match_parent"
     android:paddingLeft="@dimen/activity_horizontal_margin"
     android:paddingRight="@dimen/activity_horizontal_margin"
     android:paddingTop="@dimen/activity_vertical_margin"
     android:paddingBottom="@dimen/activity_vertical_margin"
     tools:context=".LightSwitch">
    </LinearLayout>
    ```

2. Within the preceding `LinearLayout` change the default `TextView` parameter with the following code:

    ```
    <TextView
     android:layout_width="wrap_content"
     android:layout_height="wrap_content"
     android:textAppearance="@android:style/TextAppearance.
    Large"
     android:text="Available controlled devices"/>
    ```

We create a title that we place at the top of the layout. Below this view, we will place all the available controlled devices, like our first LED.

3. Below the previous `TextView` add the following `Switch` view:

```
<Switch
  android:layout_width="wrap_content"
  android:layout_height="wrap_content"
  android:text="LED 2"
  android:id="@+id/firstLed"/>
```

To keep the user interface simple, we need a button that we can use to turn the LED on and off. For this purpose, we are going to use a switch button so that we can send the action to the microcontroller, and at the same time, give a visual feedback of what the actual LED status is.

In our Android applications, it's always a good idea to have a visual feedback about what the microcontroller is doing. In this way, we can easily know the state of the sketch and this may help us to find anomalies. This becomes relevant especially when the real-world device doesn't give any immediate feedback to the user.

Without any further customizations, the following screenshot is the expected user interface:

To try it in our board, we can proceed with the application deployment like we did in the previous chapter, and then we can proceed to write the ADK communication logic.

Android Accessory Development Kit

To enable Android ADK in our application, we need to add some configurations to our `AndroidManifest.xml` file. Because we are using a *special feature* of the Android system, which relies on the available hardware, we need to add the following declaration at the top of our `manifest` file:

```xml
<manifest
 xmlns:android="http://schemas.android.com/apk/res/android"
  package="me.palazzetti.ledlamp">

<uses-feature
android:name="android.hardware.usb.accessory"
android:required="true"/>

<!-- other declarations -->
</manifest>
```

When the application registers itself into the system, it should declare the capability to respond to events raised when a USB accessory is attached. To achieve this, we need to add an *intent filter* to our `LightSwitch` activity declaration with the highlighted code as follows:

```xml
<activity
 android:name=".LightSwitch"
 android:label="@string/app_name">
 <!-- other declarations -->

 <intent-filter>
   <action android:name=
   "android.hardware.usb.action.USB_ACCESSORY_ATTACHED"/>
 </intent-filter>
</activity>
```

The Android system requires the same accessory information that we filled in the Arduino sketch previously. Indeed, we have to provide the manufacturer, the model, and the version of our accessory, and to keep things organized, we can create the folder `res/xml/` and put inside an XML file named `usb_accessory_filter.xml`. In this file, we can add the following code:

```xml
<resources>
    <usb-accessory
     version="0.1.0"
     model="LampLed"
     manufacturer="Example, Inc."/>
</resources>
```

To include the preceding file into the Android manifest, simply add the following code below the USB intent filter:

```
<activity
 android:name=".LightSwitch"
 android:label="@string/app_name">
 <!-- other declarations -->

 <meta-data
 android:name=
 "android.hardware.usb.action.USB_ACCESSORY_ATTACHED"
 android:resource="@xml/usb_accessory_filter"/>
 </activity>
```

Now that our application is ready for the discovery process, we need to include some logic to establish the link and start to send data through the ADK.

In this prototype, we are going to use the ADK through the Android internal API. Starting from *Chapter 4, Using Sensors to Listen to the Environment*, we will use a high-level abstraction through an external library that will help us to implement our projects more easily and without any boilerplate code.

The next step is to isolate some of the ADK functionalities in a new Java package to organize our work better. We need to create a new package named adk, and we should add in it a new class called Manager. In this class, we need to use the UsbManager class that we got from the Android Context parameter, a file descriptor, and an output stream to write data in the OTG port. Add the following code in the Manager class:

```
public class Manager {
 private UsbManagermUsbManager;
 private ParcelFileDescriptormParcelFileDescriptor;
 private FileOutputStreammFileOutputStream;

 public Manager(UsbManagerusbManager) {
 this.mUsbManager = usbManager;
 }
}
```

Java snippets require many imports at the top of the file, which are intentionally missing for better code readability. However, to let everything work as expected, we need to write them and use the autocomplete function available in Android Studio. When you find a missing import, just place the cursor above the statement colored in red and press the *Ctrl+Space* keys. We can now choose the right import from the suggestion box.

We expect the `UsbManager` method as a parameter because we don't have access to the Android `Context`, and we will get it later from the main activity. To simplify our work during the ADK communication, the following helpers should be contained within our wrapper:

- `openAccessory()`: When a device is found, it should open a connection with it

- `closeAccessory()`: If any device is connected, it should close and release any used resources

- `writeSerial()`: With a connected device, it should send data through opened streams

The first helper that opens a connection with the accessory and initializes the related output stream could be realized with the following method that we should add at the bottom of the `Manager` class:

```
public void openAccessory() {
 UsbAccessory[] accessoryList = mUsbManager.getAccessoryList();
  if (accessoryList != null &&accessoryList.length> 0) {
    try {
      mDescriptor = mUsbManager.openAccessory(accessoryList[0]);
      FileDescriptor file = mDescriptor.getFileDescriptor();
      mOutput = new FileOutputStream(file);
    }
    catch (Exception e) {
      // noop
    }
  }
}
```

We are using the stored `UsbManager` object to get all the available accessories. If we have at least one accessory, we open it to initialize a descriptor and an output stream that we will use later to send data to the accessory. To close the above connection, we could add the second helper as follows:

```
public void closeAccessory() {
  if (mDescriptor != null) {
    try {
      mDescriptor.close();
    }
    catch (IOException e) {
      // noop
    }
  }
 mDescriptor = null;
}
```

If we have already opened an accessory, we use the created descriptor to close the activated streams and then we release the reference from the instance variable. Now we can add the latest write helper that includes the following code:

```
public void writeSerial(int value) {
  try {
   mOutput.write(value);
  }
 catch (IOException e) {
    // noop
  }
}
```

The preceding method writes the given `value` into the enabled output stream. In this way, if an accessory is connected, we use the output stream reference to write into the OTG port.

Finally, we need to create a `Manager` class instance in our activity, so we can use it to open a communication with Arduino. In the `onCreate` method of the `LightSwitch` activity, add the following highlighted code:

```
public class LightSwitch extends ActionBarActivity{
 private Manager mManager;

  @Override
  protected void onCreate(Bundle savedInstanceState) {
   super.onCreate(savedInstanceState);
   setContentView(R.layout.activity_light_switch);
   mManager = new Manager(
   (UsbManager) getSystemService(Context.USB_SERVICE));
  }
}
```

We are querying the system for the USB service, so we can use it inside our `Manager` class to access the state and the functions of USB accessories. We store the `Manager` class reference inside the class so that we can access our helpers in the future.

Once the `Manager` class is initialized, we should open and close our accessory contextually to the opening and the closing of the activity. Indeed, usually, it's a good idea to call the `openAccessory()` and the `closeAccessory()` functions in the activity `onResume()` and `onPause()` callbacks. In this way, we're sure that the ADK communication is initialized when we start to use it within our activity methods. To achieve this last building block to implement the ADK communication, add the following methods below the `onCreate()` member function:

```
@Override
protected void onResume() {
 super.onResume();
```

```
    mManager.openAccessory();
}

@Override
protected void onPause() {
 super.onPause();
 mManager.closeAccessory();
}
```

Now that the Android application is ready, we can proceed with the deployment, and when we disable the external OTG port, the following message appears:

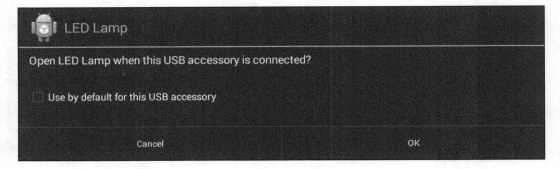

The Android system has discovered the physical accessory and is asking permission to work with it using the LED Lamp application. If we click on **OK**, the application will be opened. We can even set our application as *default*; so, whenever the accessory starts to communicate with the Android system, our application will be launched immediately.

Fast prototyping a circuit

We have a fully functional communication between Android and Arduino and now it's the time to build a real circuit. Our goal is to turn on and off an LED using the Android system and this problem is little and self-contained. However, at the beginning, we could be a little more ambitious and, instead of turning on an LED, we may want to turn on a light bulb in our bedroom. So why create such a simple project while we can make things a little more interesting? Because we are **fast prototyping** our project.

Fast prototyping is a group of techniques that we can use to create our working project as soon as possible. This is really helpful because we are removing many implementation details, such as the product design, keeping the focus only on the core of our project. In our case, we are removing all the problems related to turning on a light bulb, like the use of a transistor, a relay, and an external battery, and we're focusing on the creation of a light switch that is powered by the Android system. When the first prototype is working we can increase the requirements, step by step, until we realize the final project.

Using a breadboard

To proceed with our project, we should create a circuit prototype. We can use many tools to achieve this goal but one of the most important, at the beginning, is the **breadboard**. It can be used to connect our board and other electric components without soldering. This allows us to experiment with circuits design while reusing the breadboard for other projects.

The following is a typical breadboard:

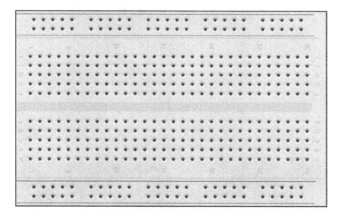

A breadboard is composed of two identical parts that are separated by a middle horizontal row that breaks any connection between the two sides. Each side contains a red and a blue row, at the top or at the bottom of the side, and they represent the *power bus*. They are connected for the whole horizontal line and we will use it to connect the power and ground of the UDOO board. The colors, usually, represent the power in red and the ground in blue, but bear in mind that this is just a convention and the colors of your breadboard may be different.

The remaining five horizontal lines are the *prototyping area* and this is where we connect our devices. Despite the power bus, these lines are connected vertically while there is no connection between the horizontal line. For instance, if we plug a **jump wire** inside the hole A1, a metal strip creates the electrical connection with the holes starting from B1 through E1. On the other hand, the holes in the range A2–E2 and F1–J1 aren't connected with our A1–E1 columns.

As our first prototype, we are going to connect our LED to our UDOO using the breadboard connections. However, we need another electric component that is called as the *resistor*. It creates an opposition to the passage of electrical current through the wire and it's necessary; otherwise, too much current can break the component. On the other hand, if we make too much electrical resistance, not enough current will flow through the component and it will not work. The electrical resistance of this component is measured in *Ohm*, and in our case, we need a *220 Ohm* resistor to power the LED correctly.

Now we need to connect our components to the breadboard as we can see in the following circuit:

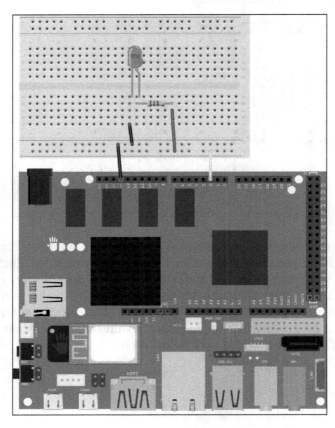

We need to connect the pinout 2 to the positive line of the power bus while the ground should be connected to the negative line. We then connect the LED into the prototyping area and put the resistor before the *positive lead*. We can distinguish the LED **polarity** *looking at its legs*: the longer leg is the positive lead while the smaller is the negative lead. Keeping this in mind, we can connect the long leg to the resistor. To close the circuit, we simply connect the resistor to the positive line of the power bus and the negative leg of the LED to the ground line. We have made our first circuit.

 The LED should be powered Off but it's possible that a small quantity of current flows through it. This could be caused by our Arduino sketch that doesn't disable the pin by default. This behavior is safe and we will manage this in the next section.

Interacting with external circuits

At this point, we have a working communication and a prototyped circuit. The last step we should achieve is to send the turn on and off signal from the Android application and to parse and execute this command in the sketch. We can start from our sketch in which we need to configure the pinout to work as an output pin. These kinds of configurations are done in the setup() function; inside it, we should add the following code:

```
void setup(){
  pinMode(LED, OUTPUT);
  digitalWrite(LED, LOW);
}
```

With the pinMode() function, we are declaring that the chosen pin will work as OUTPUT so we can control the current flow through it. Because we have previously defined the LED macro object, it refers to pin 2. The digitalWrite() function is another abstraction of the Arduino language and we use it to let current flow, or not, into the chosen pin. In this case, we are saying that no current should flow through the pin because in the initialization step, we want the LED powered off.

Because the Android application will send us a command that can have only 0 and 1 values, we need a function to parse this command so that Arduino knows what is the related action. To achieve this, we can simply add an executor() function at the bottom of our sketch as follows:

```
void executor(uint8_t command){
  switch(command) {
    case 0:
    digitalWrite(LED, LOW);
      break;
```

```
      case 1:
    digitalWrite(LED, HIGH);
       break;

    default:
      // noop
      break;
  }
}
```

We are creating a switch that parses the command parameter. If the value is 0, Arduino uses the digitalWrite() function to turn off the LED; however, if the value is 1, it uses the same function to turn the LED on. In any other case, we are just discarding the received command.

At this point, we need to put things together in our main loop() function inside the adk.isReady condition, as follows:

```
if (adk.isReady()) {
  adk.read(&bytesRead, BUFFSIZE, buffer);
  if (bytesRead> 0){
    executor(buffer[0]);
  }
}
```

During the main loop() function, if we find an ADK connection, we read any messages from the communication channel and we write the result in our buffer variable through the adk.read() function call. If we read at least 1 byte, we pass the first value of the bytes array to the executor() function. After this step, we can upload the sketch into the UDOO board.

Sending commands from Android

Now that UDOO is ready to take physical actions, we have to complete the Android application and implement the command sending within the LightSwitch class. As the first step, we need to add to our activity a variable to store the LED status. At the top of our class, add the mSwitchLed declaration:

```
private Manager mManager;
private booleanmSwitchLed = false;
```

The last thing to do is to create a method that uses the ADK writing wrapper to send a command to Arduino. Below the onCreate() method, add the following code:

```
public void switchLight(View v) {
  mSwitchLed = !mSwitchLed;
  int command = mSwitchLed ? 1 : 0;
```

```
mManager.writeSerial(command);
}
```

We are changing the state of the LED and create from it the resulting `command` parameter, which could be of `0` or `1` values. We then use the `mManager` to write the command into the OTG port. To complete the application, we just need to bind the `switchLight` method to our view. Into the `activity_light_switch.xml` file, add the `onClick()` attribute to our switch button like follows:

```
<Switch
 android:layout_width="wrap_content"
 android:layout_height="wrap_content"
 android:text="LED 2"
 android:id="@+id/firstLed"
 android:onClick="switchLight"/>
```

This was our final step and we now have our first real-world prototype. We can now upload the Android application into the UDOO board and use it to turn on and off the LED.

Summary

In this chapter, you have learned some of the UDOO characteristics related to available input and output pins, and how both processors are connected together via the internal serial bus. Moreover, in the first part, we wrote and deployed our first sketch into the board.

Then, we delved the communication mechanism realized through the ADK and wrote a new Arduino sketch capable of establishing a communication with Android using the internal OTG port. Doing the same for Android, we created a simple user interface to provide a visual feedback during the device usage. We also wrote in our Android application some wrappers to easily expose commonly used ADK methods to open and close the connection, and to write into the communication channel.

At the end of the chapter, you learned how to use a breadboard to fast prototype a circuit and you built your first one using an LED and a resistor. Then, we added all the required code to send the turn on and off signal from our Android application and to receive and execute this command from the sketch. This was a more complex Hello World application that was really helpful to build our first real-world device.

In the next chapter, we will extend the above circuit with a debugging feature so that we can test our hardware and see if our device has any broken electronic components.

3
Testing Your Physical Application

One of the most important steps during software development is **testing**. When we are testing software components, we are using a testing framework to write unit tests, and maybe integration tests, that are useful to reproduce bugs and to check the expected behavior of our application. In physical applications, this process isn't so easy because we have to test how our sketch interacts with hardware circuits.

We will add to the LedLamp application all the required features to implement an easy way to find anomalies in the circuit, so that we can avoid complex debug processes.

In this chapter, we will cover the following topics:

- Further details about electronic components and circuits
- Adding components to a circuit so they can be tested by a sketch
- Writing the first test for circuit debugging
- Running the circuit test from your prototype

Building a testable circuit

During Android application writing, we may use the internal testing framework to write instrumentation tests. With them, we can check the behavior of an application at all levels of the Android stack, including user interface stress tests. However, in our UDOO projects, we make use of Android to interact with the onboard microcontroller to control and collect data from physical devices. When we have a good features coverage through tests in our Android application, and when it matches all our requirements, it's more likely that our first problems will be related to hardware faults and anomalies.

In this book, we will not cover the Android unit testing framework because it's not required to make your first steps in hardware prototyping. However, bear in mind that you should learn how to write Android tests because it's a must to improve the quality of your software. You can find more information in the official documentation at `http://developer.android.com/training/activity-testing/index.html`.

In the previous chapter, we built our first prototype using many electronic components, such as an LED and a resistor, and we wrote an Android application to act as a devices controller. This is a good starting point, because we already have a working device in which we can add another feature. To keep the circuit simple, we will add an independent LED from the first one, to make our appliance capable of turning on and off two different devices. We need to make some changes to the LedLamp circuit to connect the second LED to the UDOO board. Take a look at the following schema:

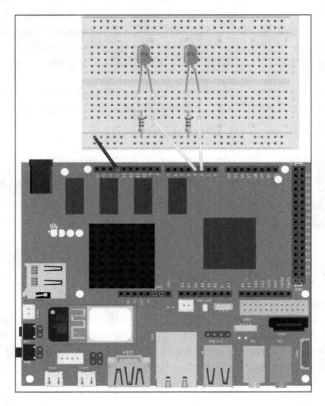

To achieve the preceding schema, take the following steps:

1. Remove the connection from the positive line of the power bus, because we need to control different components from different pins.

2. Keep the ground connected to the negative line of the power bus because we are connecting all grounds together.

3. Put two *220 Ohm resistors* to connect the negative legs to the negative power bus.

4. Connect positive legs to UDOO pinouts 2 and 3.

In the previous chapter, we connected the resistor to the positive leg, while now we are connecting the negative one. Both configurations are correct because when the LED and the resistor are connected in series, the current will flow through them with the same intensity. We can find that circuits are similar to highways, while cars are like electric charges. If cars encounter one or many roadblocks, they start to slow down at every point of the highway, and it doesn't matter if they are near or far from the roadblock. So, even if the resistor is at the end of the circuit, the right amount of current will flow through the LED.

Now that the circuit includes a new LED, we have to change our sketch so it can fit our needs with the following steps:

1. At the top of the sketch, add the following object-like macro:
   ```
   #define LED 2
   #define LED_TWO3
   ```

2. Initialize the new LED in the setup() function, as you can see in the highlighted code:
   ```
   void setup(){
     pinMode(LED, OUTPUT);
     pinMode(LED_TWO, OUTPUT);
     digitalWrite(LED, LOW);
     digitalWrite(LED_TWO, LOW);
   }
   ```

3. Add the following code to the executor() function so that the new LED behaves like the first one that we have already programmed:
   ```
   switch(command) {
     case 0:
       digitalWrite(LED, LOW);
       break;
     case 1:
       digitalWrite(LED, HIGH);
   ```

```
      break;
case 2:
  digitalWrite(LED_TWO, LOW);
  break;
case 3:
  digitalWrite(LED_TWO, HIGH);
  break;
default:
  // noop
  break;
}
```

4. Change the accessory descriptor at the top of the file to update the sketch version:

```
char versionNumber[] = "0.2.0";
```

Changing the version number is always a good practice that you should be aware of. In our case, this is also a requirement because we have to inform Android that the hardware behavior has changed. As you saw in *Chapter 2, Know your Tools*, when versions defined in Android and Arduino mismatch, the Android application will not communicate with the microcontroller, and this prevents unexpected behaviors, especially when the hardware is changed. Indeed, if we deploy the new sketch again, we can see that Android will not find any available application to manage the accessory.

The last step where the prototype will work again, is to update the Android application starting from its user interface and logic, so that it becomes capable to manage the new device. To achieve this goal, we should take the following steps:

1. Add a new switch button into `res/layout/activity_light_switch.xml` file, below the `firstLed` declaration:

```
<Switch
 android:layout_width="wrap_content"
 android:layout_height="wrap_content"
 android:text="LED 3"
 android:id="@+id/secondLed"
 android:onClick="switchLightTwo"/>
```

2. Add in the `LightSwitch` activity at the top of the class, the following declaration to store the state of the second LED:

```
private boolean mSwitchLed = false;
private boolean mSwitchLedTwo = false;
```

3. Add the following code under the `switchLight()` method to pilot the second LED according to the sketch switch case:

```
public void switchLightTwo(View v) {
 mSwitchLedTwo = !mSwitchLedTwo;
 int command = mSwitchLedTwo ? 3 : 2;
 mManager.writeSerial(command);
}
```

4. Update the `usb_accessory_filter.xml` descriptor file under `res/xml/` with the new hardware version:

```
<resources>
 <usb-accessory
 version="0.2.0"
 model="LedLamp"
 manufacturer="Example, Inc."/>
</resources>
```

We are matching the version of the sketch so Android knows that this application can manage the connected accessory again. After deploying the new application, we can use the prototype to turn on and off the two connected LEDs.

Developing a diagnostic mode

With a working prototype, it's time to add a functionality that we can use to test our circuit. Even if we are tempted to put our hands on code, we need first to simulate a physical damage that causes a fault in the prototype. Because we don't want to really damage one of our LEDs, we can always alter the circuit components to reproduce an anomaly.

Indeed, we can simulate that the resistor connected to pin 3 has a broken leg. If this occurs, the circuit is interrupted and this prevents the current from flowing through the LED. To reproduce this problem in our breadboard, we can simply remove the first resistor, as we can see in the following schema:

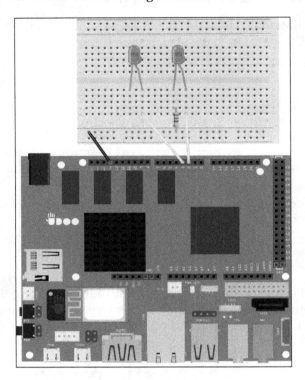

Now we have simulated our first hardware fault. If we open the Android application and use the on/off switches, we can see that the second LED works as expected while the first one stops working. However, none of the software components notice anything because they are agnostic to what happens under the hood. If such problems occurs, we are lost because we start software and hardware debugging without knowing in which part we should put our attention to find the fault.

When the software doesn't work, we usually use a debugger. Unfortunately, when we deal with electric circuits, we don't have so many tools and we may need to implement something on our own. A good starting point is to add a functionality to the prototype so it can debug itself through a **diagnostic** mode. This mode should *simulate and mimic the real behaviors of our circuit*, but in a controlled way. Diagnostic mode is really helpful to identify the cause of anomalies in our prototype when the problem is not related to a software bug.

The diagnostic mode is the first step we should follow to find anomalies. However, when we find a hardware fault, we should start using other tools such as a *multimeter*, which has the capability to measure voltage, current, and resistance.

Before we start to implement this mode in our sketch, we need to connect a *push button* that we will use to enable the diagnostic mode. We need to add this component to our breadboard, as you can see in the left part of the following schema:

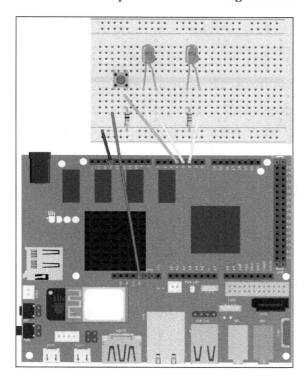

The procedure to add components to the breadboard, as shown in the schema, is as follows:

1. Add the push button to the middle of our breadboard so that the legs in the same vertical line aren't connected.

2. Connect the left leg of the button to pin +5V.

3. Connect the right leg of the button to pin 4.

4. Connect one side of a *10 KOhm* resistor to the right leg of the button and the other side to the negative line of the power bus.

Through these connections, we read a digital signal from pin 4 when we press the push button because the *current chooses the path with lesser resistance*, like water does. In our case, the mechanical switch will create a connection between the +5V and the 4 pins, and because the resistance of this path is greatly inferior to the *10 KOhm* present in the ground path, UDOO will read this voltage difference and convert it into a digital signal. When the switch is open, the only available path is pin 4 and the ground so UDOO reads no voltage differences. This allows us to know whether the switch is pressed or not.

Writing the first test

Now that we have a physical hardware switch, we need to activate the diagnostic mode when users press the push button. To detect the button press, we should change the sketch according to the following steps:

1. Add the highlighted declarations, just after the ADK initialization:

    ```
    ADKadk(&Usb, manufacturer, model, accessoryName, versionNumber,
    url, serialNumber);
    int reading = LOW;
    int previous = LOW;
    long lastPress = 0;
    ```

    We need the button state for each reading phase so that we can save the state during the current and the previous reading. The lastPress variable will contain the timestamp when the button was pressed last time. We set the button status to LOW because we state that no current flows through the button and this means that it's not pressed.

2. At the top of the sketch, define the following object-like macros:

    ```
    #define LED_TWO3
    #define BUTTON 4
    #define DEBOUNCE 200
    ```

    We set the BUTTON pin 4 and a DEBOUNCE value that refers to the number of milliseconds that should elapse before our code starts to evaluate the button press again. The use of this threshold is required because it prevents the reading of false positive. If we omit this part, when the button is pressed, the sketch will detect thousands of readings because the UDOO reading phase is faster than our reaction to release the push button. This value is called **debounce threshold**.

3. Configure the button pin mode in the setup() function as follows:

    ```
    pinMode(LED_TWO, OUTPUT);
    pinMode(BUTTON, INPUT);
    ```

4. Move the content of the `loop()` function into a new one called the `readCommand()` function so that it matches the following:

```
void readCommand() {
 Usb.Task();
 if (adk.isReady()) {
   adk.read(&bytesRead, BUFFSIZE, buffer);
   if (bytesRead> 0) {
     executor(buffer[0]);
   }
 }
}
```

5. With an empty `loop()` function, we should add in it the reading phase with the following code:

```
void loop(){
  // Reads the digital signal from the circuit
  reading = digitalRead(BUTTON);
  // Checks the button press if it's outside a
  // debounce threshold
  if (reading == HIGH && previous == LOW &&millis() -
  lastPress>DEBOUNCE) {
    lastPress = millis();
     // Visual effect prior to diagnostic activation
    digitalWrite(LED, HIGH);
    digitalWrite(LED_TWO, HIGH);
    delay(500);
    digitalWrite(LED, LOW);
    digitalWrite(LED_TWO, LOW);
    delay(500);
    startDiagnostic();
  }
  previous = reading;
  readCommand();
}
```

We are storing the value of the button using the built-in `digitalRead()` function, which abstracts the complexity to read the voltage difference from the chosen pin. Then, we are checking if the current state is different from the previous, so we are sure that the button is pressed exactly in this moment.

However, we also need to check whether the time since we press the push button exceeds the debounce threshold. We use the built-in `millis()` function, which returns the number of milliseconds since the UDOO board has started the current program.

If the press button event is caught, we set the `lastPress` value and show a visual feedback to notify users that the diagnostic mode is about to start. In any case, we are saving the previous button state and continuing with the standard execution.

> Sometimes the diagnostic mode requires activation and deactivation phases. In our case, we are keeping the process simple so the diagnostic mode runs only once after the button is pressed. In other projects, we may need a more complex activation mechanism that we can isolate in a standalone function.

6. As a last step, implement the `startDiagnostic()` function as follows:

```
void startDiagnostic() {
  // Turn on the first LED
  executor(1);
  delay(1000);
  executor(0);
  // Turn on the second LED
  executor(3);
  delay(1000);
  executor(2);
  // Turn on both
  executor(1);
  executor(3);
  delay(1000);
  executor(0);
  executor(2);
}
```

The diagnostic function should mimic all, or almost all, possible behaviors of our circuit. In this case, we turn on and off the first and the second LED and, as the last test, we power them on together. In a diagnostic mode, it's important to use internal functions to reproduce the circuit actions. This helps us to test the `executor()` function's inputs so that we are sure that we have mapped all expected inputs sent by the Android application.

Now that we have a diagnostic function, we have to deploy our LedLamp sketch once again and push the button to start the diagnosis. As expected, only one LED should turn on because of the virtually broken resistor. Now we can connect the resistor again and start the diagnostic mode to test if the LED connection has been fixed.

Summary

In this chapter, we have delved into hardware testing to enhance the quality of our projects. We found how valuable this process is because, with this approach, we can isolate hardware faults from software bugs.

We added another LED to our previous prototype so that we can control multiple devices from the Android application. Then, we simulated a hardware fault in one of the electric components, removing one resistor from the circuit to produce a controlled anomaly. This led us to write our own diagnostic mode to find these kinds of faults quickly.

The first step was to add a push button to our prototype that we can use to start the diagnostic mode and then we used this functionality to mimic all the possible circuit behaviors to find the broken resistor easily.

In the next chapter, we start a new prototype from scratch, which is capable of collecting data from the environment, through a new set of electronic components. We will also write an Android application capable of reading these values sent from the sketch and to visualize the processed data.

4
Using Sensors to Listen to the Environment

When we are building our prototypes, we want to provide the best possible interaction for our final users. Sometimes, we build real-world applications that don't have any human interaction but they simply listen to the environment to collect data and decide what to do. Whatever our prototype, if we want to read and understand human actions or environment changes, we need to use a new set of electronic components: **sensors**.

Every time we build a physical application, we have to bear in mind that the more complex our project is, the more likely we need to add sensors to achieve the desired interaction.

In this chapter, we will start a new real-world application from scratch that is capable of sensing our heartbeat and publishing the result to our Android application.

In this chapter, we will cover the following topics:

- Working with environment sensors
- Building a heartbeat monitor
- Collecting data from sensors
- Showing collected data from an Android application

Working with environment sensors

In electronics, sensors are components built *to detect any changes* of a particular matter or particle property. When any change occurs, the sensor provides a voltage variation that can change the current flow and behavior of other electric components. If a microcontroller is connected to a sensor, it can decide to take different actions according to the running program.

Sensors can detect changes in many *properties*, such as heat radiation, humidity, light, radio, sound waves, and many others. When we are using a sensor in our projects, we have to choose a particular property to listen to and then we need to read and manage the voltage variation. Sometimes, to perform our checks, we need to transform these electrical changes into other measurement units, such as meters or temperature's degree. At other times, we may use more complex sensors that already make a total or a partial conversion for us. For example, if we are building a robot rover, we may need to use a sensor to detect the distance from an object in order to dodge any room obstacles. In this case, we will use an *ultrasonic sensor* that is based on a principle similar to radar or sonar. It emits high frequency sound waves and evaluates the echo that is received. Analyzing the time interval between sending and receiving the signal echo, we can determinate the distance from an object.

Indeed, in a generic sketch, we read the elapsed microseconds from the sensor before the signal echo is received. To make these values more useful and to find the right distance, we may need to write a microsecond to centimeters or inches converter inside the sketch.

However, this is possible only if we know how the sensor works and how many centimeters or inches are traveled by the signal for each microsecond. Fortunately, we can find this information in a document released by the component manufacturer, which is called a **datasheet**. With this knowledge, we can easily convert all probed values into what we are looking for. When we finish the prototype in this chapter, we could take a look at the URL `http://arduino.cc/en/tutorial/ping`, which includes an example about how to use an ultrasonic sensor and how it's easy to convert the detected signal into a different measurement unit.

Building a heartbeat monitor

In the previous chapters, we built our first prototype equipped with an LED actuator to alter the surround environment, and then we enabled the Android application to control the LED behavior through the internal ADK communication. We have seen that sensors are really helpful to improve interactions of our prototypes and we may be tempted to add this new capability to the previous project. Indeed, because we're using a component capable of producing light, we may think about adding an external light sensor so that the microcontroller is capable of turning on and off the LED according to the environment light.

This is just an example of how we can use a light sensor. Indeed, we have to bear in mind that each sensor can be used in different ways and it's our job to find a correlation between detected values and the goal of our physical application. We should never stop to use sensors only for their main use, as we will see in the heartbeat monitor.

Creating a circuit with a light sensor

Similar to the previous prototypes, the heartbeat monitor is composed of two parts. The first one is the circuit and the sketch that should collect data from the light sensor and convert it into a value that represents the **beats per minute (bpm)**. The second is the Android application, which shows the computed value of our heart rate on the screen.

 Even if this prototype could achieve good results, it's always a bad idea to use homemade prototypes for medical reasons. The photoresistor is used only for a demonstration and *should not* be used for any medical purposes.

For this physical application, we are going to use a **photoresistor** as a part of our light sensor. A photoresistor, also called **Light Dependent Resistor (LDR)**, works like a traditional resistor used in previous prototypes, but it's slightly different regarding how much resistance it provides. Indeed, its resistance is variable according to measured light intensity and if we monitor this value, we can easily calculate whether the environment intensity is increasing or decreasing. We also use a *bright red* LED, which is different from the one used before because it's powerful enough to let the light pass through our skin.

Our goal is to create a circuit where we can put one side of our index finger at the top of the photoresistor, and the bright LED on the other side. In this way, a part of the light will pass through our finger and will be detected by the photoresistor. During every heartbeat, a pressure wave moves out along the arteries increasing our blood volume. When the light goes through our tissues, this blood volume variation changes the quantity of light that falls on the sensor. So, when we see medium or high changes in the probed values, probably, this is our heartbeat.

To begin the construction of our prototype, we need to put the photoresistor into our breadboard so that we can achieve the following schema:

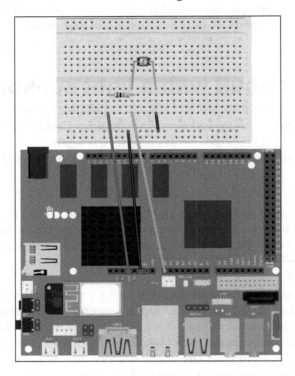

Go through the following steps to achieve the preceding schema:

1. The photoresistor may have legs that are too long. Use an electronics component cutter to cut the legs so that they are, at most, 1.5cm. This is not a requirement but it could simplify the use of the prototype.

2. Connect the UDOO +3.3V pin to the first line of the breadboard. Be sure not to connect the +5V power pin because it may damage the board during connections.

3. Put a *10 KOhm* resistor on the board and connect it to the +3.3V pin; we also need to connect the other lead to the analog input A0 pin.

4. Connect the photoresistor to the same column of the resistor and the A0 pin; the second lead should be connected to the negative line of the power bus.

[Photoresistors act like any other resistors, so it's not important which lead we connect on this step because *they have no polarity*.]

5. Connect UDOO ground to the negative line of the power bus.

With these steps, we built a **voltage divider** circuit composed of two resistors. These kinds of circuit produce an output voltage, which is a fraction of the input voltage according to the resistance values. This means that, because the resistance is variable according to the light intensity, the voltage divider gives an output voltage that changes with illumination. In this way, the board notices the changes and transforms them in a numeric value, in a range between 0 and 1023. In other words, when the photoresistor is in the shade, we read a high value, while when it's in the light, we read a low value. Because we connect the *10 KOhm* resistor to the +3.3V pin, we can state that this voltage divider has been built using a **pull-up** resistor.

Voltage divers are commonly used in many electronic circuits. You can find more information about other applications of this kind of circuit at https://learn.sparkfun.com/tutorials/voltage-dividers.

To complete our prototype, we have to add the bright LED to the circuit. However, because we need to put the LED on the opposite side of our finger, we can't connect the component directly to our breadboard, but we need to use a couple of *crocodile clips*. As a first step, we need to extend the circuit as per the following schema:

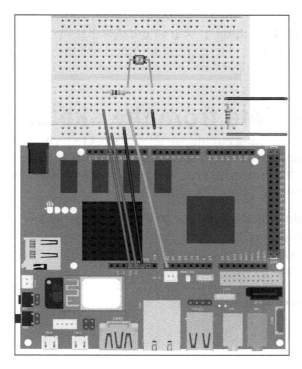

Go through the following steps to achieve the preceding schema:

1. Connect the UDOO +5V power pin to the positive line of the power bus.

2. Add a *220 Ohm* resistor to the breadboard and connect one lead to the negative line of the power bus.

3. Connect one side of a wire connector to the other lead of the *220 Ohm* resistor.

4. Connect one side of a wire connector to the positive line of the power bus.

5. Connect one side of the first crocodile clip to the wire connected to the positive line of the power bus.

6. Connect one side of the second crocodile clip to the wire connected to the resistor.

7. Connect the crocodile clip that extends the +5V pin to the long leg of the LED.

> Before proceeding with the next step, remember that you're using a really bright LED. You should avoid directing it at your eyes.

8. Connect the crocodile clip that extends the resistor and the ground connection to the short leg of the LED.

If all the connections are set, the LED should turn on and we can use it as a moving part of our prototype. One thing to bear in mind is that the metal terminal ends of the crocodile clips *should never touch together* otherwise the circuit will stop working and some components may get damaged because of a *short circuit*.

Collecting data from the sketch

Now that we have a working circuit, we should start to write down our sketch to collect data from the light sensor. Then we should analyze these results and think about an algorithm to transform readings into a heartbeat counter. We should start a new sketch and add the following steps:

1. Add the following declarations on the top of the sketch:

```
#define SENSOR A0
#define HEARTBEAT_POLL_PERIOD50
#define SECONDS 10
constint TIMESLOTS = SECONDS * 1000 / HEARTBEAT_POLL_PERIOD;
int sensorReading = 0;
```

We define the object-like macro SENSOR with a A0 value that is the pin we will use for the analog read. We set HEARTBEAT_POLL_PERIOD to specify how many milliseconds the microcontroller should wait between consecutive sensor readings. With the SECONDS parameter, we define the seconds that should elapse before we use collected data to process and estimate the heart rate. Indeed, we multiply SECONDS by 1000 to convert this value into milliseconds and then we divide it by the HEARTBEAT_POLL_PERIOD parameter to define the TIMESLOTS constant. This variable defines how many times we should loop the reading phase to collect the right number of readings to estimate the heart rate. In this way, we make a read for each TIMESLOTS cycle and when the cycle ends, we calculate the heart rate. The last variable sensorReading is used to store the sensor reading during each loop iteration.

2. In the setup() function, add the initialization of the serial port so that we can open a communication between the UDOO board and our computer:

```
void setup() {
  Serial.begin(115200);
}
```

3. Add the following function at the bottom of the sketch to print read values through the serial port:

```
void printRawData() {
  sensorReading = analogRead(SENSOR);
  Serial.println(sensorReading);
}
```

We use the analogRead built-in function to read the incoming data from the analog input pin. Because these pins are read-only, we don't need to do any further configuration in the setup() function or to change the input resolution.

 Sometimes we may need a better analog read resolution with a range between 0 and 4095 instead of 0 and 1023. In this case, we should change the resolution using the analogReadResolution parameter. We can find more information about the analog input resolution in the official documentation at http://arduino.cc/en/Reference/AnalogReadResolution.

When the read is complete, we print the result in the serial port so that we can read these values through the Arduino IDE serial monitor.

4. In the main `loop()` function, add the `printRawData()` function call for each reading timeslot:

```
void loop() {
  for (int j = 0; j < TIMESLOTS; j++) {
    printRawData();
    delay(HEARTBEAT_POLL_PERIOD);
  }
  Serial.println("Done!");
  delay(1000);
}
```

We are making the TIMESLOTS iterations so that we can get readings for 10 seconds, as defined earlier. After all the readings are done, we print a message on the serial port and wait for a second before starting again with the readings.

> The delay of a second and the **Done!** message are only proof of the concept that the reading cycle is working correctly. We will remove them later.

After this configuration, we can upload the sketch and proceed with our first experiment. Put the bottom side of your index finger on the photoresistor while the LED is put on the other side.

> To get finer readings, it's better if the contact part with the photoresistor and the LED is the part between the phalanx and the nail.

To start the experiment, click on the **Serial Monitor** button and when the sketch prints the **Done!** message, we will see some values as shown in the following screenshot:

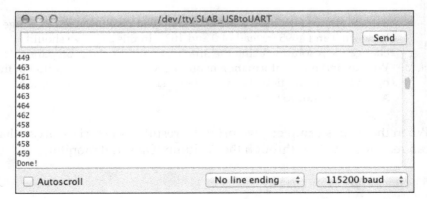

These are the absolute values that the light sensor caught during our heartbeats. If we copy and paste a full 10 seconds iteration into Microsoft Excel, Libre Office Calc, or Numbers spreadsheet, we can draw a line chart and see the given results in a more understandable format:

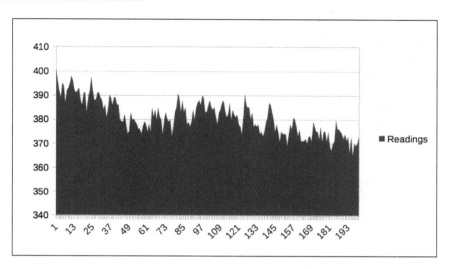

We can see that the values change over time, and when a heartbeat occurs, the light sensor detects a variation of the light intensity and this event causes a peak in our chart. In other words, we can assume that every peak is related to a single heartbeat. The next step is to improve our sketch to approximate and convert these values, because we should try to remove reading errors and false positives. The main idea is to collect a fixed number of samples after each iteration to store the difference between this reading and the last one. If we store all differences over the time, we can easily find the trend of our readings and recognize when we read a peak. To improve our algorithm, we need to perform the following steps:

1. Add the following variables on the top of the sketch:

```
#define SECONDS 10
#define SAMPLES 10

constint TIMESLOTS = SECONDS * 1000 /
HEARTBEAT_POLL_PERIOD;

int sensorReading = 0;
int lastReading = 0;
int readings[SAMPLES];
int i = 0;
int delta = 0;
int totalReading = 0;
```

We set how many SAMPLES we use to calculate the incremental differences. We then use lastReading, i, and delta variables to store respectively the last reading, the current index to iterate the readings array and the current difference from the last reading. We then define an accumulator to store the current total reading.

2. Initialize the readings array in the setup function:

```
void setup() {
 Serial.begin(115200);

 for (int j = 0; j < SAMPLES; j++) {
   readings[j] = 0;
 }
}
```

3. Add the collectReads() function at the bottom of the sketch:

```
void collectReads() {
 sensorReading = analogRead(SENSOR);
  delta = sensorReading - lastReading;
 lastReading = sensorReading;
 totalReading = totalReading - readings[i] + delta;
  readings[i] = delta;
 i = (i + 1) % SAMPLES;
}
```

In the first part we are going to read the current value and calculate the difference from the last reading. Then we accumulate this difference using the current totalReading and the last stored difference in the readings array. We can now update the readings array with the new delta object for the current index, which is incremented in the last line and is kept within bounds using the *modulo operator.*

4. In the main loop() function, substitute the printRawData() function call with the new collectReads() function and then print the accumulated value:

```
for (int j = 0; j < TIMESLOTS; j++) {
 collectReads();
 Serial.println(totalReading);
  delay(HEARTBEAT_POLL_PERIOD);
}
```

With these enhancements, we can upload the new sketch and repeat the experiment in the same way we did previously:

1. Put your index finger between the photoresistor and the LED.
2. Click on **serial monitor** on the Arduino IDE.
3. Complete a full 10 seconds iteration.
4. Copy and paste the values into the previous spreadsheet and draw a bar chart. We should avoid including the first eight readings because they are related to the first iteration where the readings array is not initialized yet.

The collected values produce a chart, as follows:

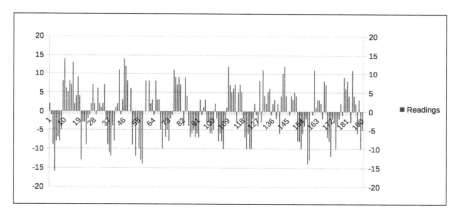

In these processed readings, there are fluctuations between positive and negative values and this occurs when we are climbing or descending the peaks we saw in the first chart. With this knowledge, we can improve a little of our algorithm so that we can track the climbing or descending phase and choose whether to discard the reading or count it as a single heartbeat. To complete this part, we need to add the following code using the following steps:

1. Add these declarations at the top of the sketch:

```
#define SECONDS 10
#define POS_THRESHOLD 3
#define NEG_THRESHOLD -3

const int TIMESLOTS = SECONDS * 1000 / HEARTBEAT_POLL_PERIOD;
const int PERMINUTE = 60 / SECONDS;
int beats = 0;
boolean hillClimb = false;
```

We define the POS_THRESHOLD and NEG_THRESHOLD parameters to set the bounds of the interval in which we discard values to avoid false positives. We also define a PERMINUTE constant to know which is the multiplier to get the beats per minute and the beats accumulator. As a last declaration, we set the hillClimb variable to store if the next readings are in the ascending or descending phase. For instance, a True value means that we are in the ascending phase.

2. Add the findBeat() function at the bottom of the sketch:

```
void findBeat() {
  if (totalReading<NEG_THRESHOLD) {
  hillClimb = true;
  }
  if ((totalReading>POS_THRESHOLD)&&hillClimb) {
  hillClimb = false;
    beats += 1;
  }
}
```

We check whether the totalReading parameter is below NEG_THRESHOLD parameter to know whether we are in the descending phase of a peak. In this case, we set the hillClimb variable to True. In the last code block, we check whether we are over the POS_THRESHOLD and in the ascending phase. In that case, we set the hillClimb to False and count this phase change as a heartbeat. If we take a look at the previous chart, through the preceding code we can easily determine in which phase we are during each reading, and with this information we can discard as many errors and false positives as possible.

3. Add the utility function calcHeartRate() at the bottom of the sketch:

```
int calcHeartRate() {
  return beats * PERMINUTE;
}
```

4. In the main loop() function, add the following code to use the previous functions and to print the heart rate with the number of beats in the serial port:

```
for (int j = 0; j < TIMESLOTS; j++) {
 collectReads();
 findBeat();
  delay(HEARTBEAT_POLL_PERIOD);
}
Serial.print(calcHeartRate());
Serial.print(" with: ");
Serial.println(beats);
beats = 0;
delay(1000);
```

5. Upload the sketch again and start to count the heartbeats. In the serial monitor, we will notice the following values:

```
72 with: 12
84 with: 14
66 with: 11
78 with: 13
90 with: 15
84 with: 14
```

The last improvement for our sketch is to add the ADK functionalities to send computed heartbeats to our Android application. At the top of the sketch, add the following *accessory descriptor*, which is almost equal to the one we used in the previous prototypes:

```
#include <adk.h>
#define BUFFSIZE 128
char accessoryName[] = "Heartbeat monitor";
char manufacturer[] = "Example, Inc.";
char model[] = "HeartBeat";
char versionNumber[] = "0.1.0";
char serialNumber[] = "1";
char url[] = "http://www.example.com";
uint8_t buffer[BUFFSIZE];
uint32_tbytesRead = 0;
USBHostUsb;
ADKadk(&Usb, manufacturer, model, accessoryName,
versionNumber, url, serialNumber);
```

As the last step, in the main `loop()` function, wrap the sketch execution in the ADK communication and remove all serial prints together with the last delay of a second:

```
void loop() {
Usb.Task();
  if (adk.isReady()) {
    // Collect data
    for (int j = 0; j < TIMESLOTS; j++) {
      collectReads();
      findBeat();
      delay(HEARTBEAT_POLL_PERIOD);
    }
  buffer[0] = calcHeartRate();
  adk.write(1, buffer);
  beats = 0;
  }
}
```

In this way, the heart rate monitor will start when the ADK communication is up and running and we will use the `adk.write()` function to send the computed heart rate back to the Android application.

Android for data visualization

Now that our physical application has a fully working circuit to read our heart rate through an unconventional use of a light sensor, we should complete the prototype with an Android application. From the Android Studio, start a new Android project called *HeartMonitor* with **Android API 19**. During the bootstrap process, choose a **Blank Activity** named *Monitor*.

We start writing the application from the user interface, and we have to think and design the activity layout. For the purpose of this application, we write a simple layout with a title and a text component that we will update every time Android receives a heartbeat estimation from the sketch. This layout could be achieved through the following steps:

1. In the `styles.xml` file under `res/values/`, add these color declarations and replace the standard theme:

   ```
   <color name="sulu">#CBE86B</color>
   <color name="bright_red">#A30006</color>

   <style name="AppTheme" parent="Theme.AppCompat">
   <!-- Customize your theme here. -->
   </style>
   ```

   The `AppTheme` parameter inherits the `Theme.AppCompat` parameter that refers to the *Holo Dark* theme available in the Android support library. We also create green and red colors that we will use later in our application.

2. In the `activity_monitor.xml` file under `res/layout/`, replace the root layout with the highlighted changes:

   ```
   <LinearLayout
   xmlns:android="http://schemas.android.com/apk/res/
   android"
     xmlns:tools="http://schemas.android.com/tools"
     android:orientation="vertical"
     android:layout_width="match_parent"
     android:layout_height="match_parent"
     android:paddingLeft="@dimen/activity_horizontal_margin"
     android:paddingRight="@dimen/activity_horizontal_margin"
     android:paddingTop="@dimen/activity_vertical_margin"
     android:paddingBottom="@dimen/activity_vertical_margin"
     tools:context=".Monitor">

   </LinearLayout>
   ```

3. Change the `TextView` parameter included in the preceding layout with the following code to have a bigger green title that will show the application name:

```
<TextView
  android:text="Android heart rate monitor"
  android:gravity="center"
  android:textColor="@color/sulu"
  android:textSize="30sp"
  android:layout_width="match_parent"
  android:layout_height="wrap_content" />
```

4. Nest a new `LinearLayout` in the root layout:

```
<LinearLayout
  android:layout_width="match_parent"
  android:layout_height="wrap_content"
  android:layout_marginTop="30sp"
  android:gravity="center">
</LinearLayout>
```

We set a margin from the previous element, using all available space to place the inner components in a center position.

5. Add the following TextViews to show the label and the placeholder that will contain the computed beats per minute:

```
<TextView
  android:text="Current heartbeat: "
  android:textColor="@color/sulu"
  android:textSize="20sp"
  android:layout_width="wrap_content"
  android:layout_height="wrap_content"/>

<TextView
  android:id="@+id/bpm"
  android:text="0 bpm"
  android:textColor="@color/bright_red"
  android:textSize="20sp"
  android:layout_width="wrap_content"
  android:layout_height="wrap_content"/>
```

6. Retrieve the widget within the activity class in order to change it after each reading. Add the following declaration at the top of the `Monitor` class:

```
private TextViewmBpm;
```

7. Find the view identified by the `bpm` identifier in the `onCreate()` callback through the highlighted code:

```
@Override
protected void onCreate(Bundle savedInstanceState) {
  super.onCreate(savedInstanceState);
  setContentView(R.layout.activity_monitor);
  mBpm = (TextView) findViewById(R.id.bpm);
}
```

Without any further configuration, the following is the obtained layout:

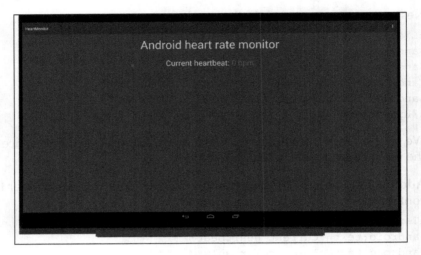

The application layout is now complete and we can proceed to setup the ADK communication.

Setting up the ADKToolkit

Like we did for the first prototype, we need to write all ADK classes and methods again to send and receive data. However, because a good principle of software development is Don't repeat yourself (DRY), we are going to use an external library that provides a high abstraction for all needed functionalities. The library is called **ADKToolkit** and it's a wrapper for the native ADK APIs that prevents code duplication every time we start a new project. We can find more information and examples related to the library at `http://docs.adktoolkit.org`.

The first step that is required is to add the ADKToolkit library to the application dependencies. In the projects built with Android Studio, we have two different files called `build.gradle`. These files contain all the configurations related to the Gradle build system, and one of them is related to the global project, while the other is related to the module application we're building. Even if both the files contain a list of dependencies, we should add the library to the `build.gradle` file related to the application module, which is located in the app folder. If we're using the **Project** panel available on the left of the Android Studio interface, we have to double-click on the **build.gradle (Module: app)** script. In this file, we need to add the highlighted code within the `dependencies` block:

```
dependencies {
  compile fileTree(dir: 'libs', include: ['*.jar'])
  compile 'com.android.support:appcompat-v7:21.0.3'
  compile 'me.palazzetti:adktoolkit:0.3.0'
}
```

Now we can click on the **Sync Now** button available in the flash message and wait for gradle to complete the synchronization process that downloads the ADKToolkit library automatically.

Like we did in *Chapter 2*, *Know your Tools*, we should update the Android manifest file to register the application with the correct intent filter and accessory descriptor. To proceed with the ADK configuration, follow these reminders:

1. Create the accessory filter file `usb_accessory_filter.xml` located under `res/xml/` with the following code:

```
<resources>
 <usb-accessory
    version="0.1.0"
    model="HeartBeat"
    manufacturer="Example, Inc."/>
</resources>
```

2. Add the USB `<uses-feature>` tag in the `AndroidManifest.xml` file.

3. In the activity block of the `AndroidManifest.xml` file, add the ADK `<intent-filter>` and the `<meta-data>` tags to set the USB accessory filter.

Now we must initialize the ADKToolkit library to enable the communication and start reading processed data. In the `Monitor` class, add the following snippets:

1. Declare the `AdkManager` object at the top of the class:

```
private TextViewmBpm;
private AdkManagermAdkManager;
```

2. Add the `AdkManager` initialization in the `onCreate()` method:

```
mBpm = (TextView) findViewById(R.id.bpm);
mAdkManager = new AdkManager(this);
```

The `AdkManager` is the main class of the ADKToolkit library. To initialize the manager instance, we should pass the current context to its constructor, and because the activity class inherits from `Context` class, we can simply pass the instance using the `this` keyword. All functionalities related to the ADK communication will be used through the `mAdkManager` instance.

3. Override the `onResume()` and `onPause()` callbacks to start and stop the ADK connection when the `Monitor` activity is opening or closing:

```
@Override
protected void onResume() {
  super.onResume();
  mAdkManager.open();
}

@Override
 protected void onPause() {
  super.onPause();
  mAdkManager.close();
}
```

The `mAdkManager` instance exposes the `close()` and `open()` methods to control easily the accessory connection. We have to bear in mind that it's a requirement to open the ADK communication in the `onResume()` method, because the `AdkManager` initialization is not sufficient to enable the channel between Android and Arduino.

With the previous steps, we have completed the ADK configuration and now we can start to write the logic to receive data from the sketch.

Continuous data readings from Android

The main concept of our Android application is to use the ADKToolkit to make continuous readings of data collected by UDOO board. Every time estimations are written in the OTG serial port, we need to read these values and update the Android user interface, but, before we proceed, we need to make some considerations about the Android threading system.

When an Android application starts, all the components of this application run in the same process and thread. This is called the **main thread** and it hosts among other components, the current foreground `Activity` instance. Whenever we need to update any views of the current activity, we should run the updating code in the main thread, otherwise the application will crash. On the other hand, we have to bear in mind that any operation done in the main thread should be completed immediately. If our code is slow or if it makes blocking operations such as I/O, the system that will popup the **Application Not Responding** (**ANR**) dialog because the main thread is unable to handle user input events.

This error will surely occur if we run continuous readings in the main thread, because we should query the light sensor in a cycle, which causes blocking I/O operations every 10 seconds. For these reasons, we can make use of an `ExecutorService` class that can run periodical scheduled threads. In our case, we will define a short-lived thread that will be created every 10 seconds from the above scheduler.

When the scheduled thread finishes reading data from the OTG serial port, it should communicate the received message to the main thread through a `Handler` class. We can find more information and examples about how to communicate with the main thread in the official Android documentation at:

`https://developer.android.com/training/multiple-threads/communicate-ui.html`.

As a first step we should expose all the required methods to update the Android user interface through the following steps:

1. Create a new Java interface called `OnDataChanges` and add the following method:

    ```
    public interface OnDataChanges {
      void updateBpm(byte heartRate);
    }
    ```

    Through this code, we define the interface that we will use in our `Handler` to update the user interface with the given `heartRate` parameter.

2. Implement the interface in the `Monitor` class through the highlighted code:

```
public class Monitor extends ActionBarActivity implements
OnDataChanges {
  private TextViewmBpm;
  // ...
```

3. Write the following code at the end of the class to update the Android user interface through the `updateBpm` method:

```
@Override
public void updateBpm(byte heartRate) {
 mBpm.setText(String.format("%d bpm", heartRate));
 }
```

The last required step is to implement our scheduled thread that reads processed data from Arduino and writes these values in the user interface. To complete this last building block, perform the following steps:

1. Create a new package in your namespace called `adk`.

2. In the `adk` package, add a new class named `DataReader`.

3. At the top of the class, add the following declarations:

```
private final static int HEARTBEAT_POLLING = 10000;
private final static int HEARTBEAT_READ = 0;
private AdkManager mAdkManager;
private OnDataChanges mCaller;
private ScheduledExecutorService mScheduler;
private Handler mMainLoop;
```

We're defining the heartbeat polling time and an `int` variable that we use later to identify the published message within our handler. We also store the references for the `AdkManager` parameter and the `caller` activity to use the ADK `read` method and the `updateBpm` callback, respectively. Then we define our `ExecutorService` implementation together with a `Handler` that we will attach to the main thread.

4. Implement the `DataReader` constructor to define the handling message code when the main thread receives a new message from the background thread:

```
public DataReader(AdkManageradkManager, OnDataChanges
caller) {
 this.mAdkManager = adkManager;
 this.mCaller = caller;
 mMainLoop = new Handler(Looper.getMainLooper()) {
    @Override
    public void handleMessage(Message message) {
```

```
      switch (message.what) {
        case HEARTBEAT_READ:
    mCaller.updateBpm((byte) message.obj);
          break;
      }
    }
  };
}
```

After storing the `AdkManager` instance and `caller` activity references, we attach a new `Handler` to the application's main looper, which lives in the main thread. We should override the `handleMessage` callback in order to check the user defined message code to identify the `HEARTBEAT_READ` message. In this case, we call the `updateBpm` callback using the object attached to the received `message` parameter.

 Each `Handler` has its own namespace for message codes, so you do not need to worry about your `message.what` attribute's possible values conflicting with the other handlers.

5. At the bottom of the `DataReader` class, add the following private class that implements the `Runnable` interface to read and publish sensor data:

```java
private class SensorThread implements Runnable {
  @Override
  public void run() {
    // Read from ADK
   AdkMessage response = mAdkManager.read();
    // ADK response back to UI thread for update
    Message message = mMainLoop.obtainMessage(HEARTBEAT_READ,
    response.getByte());
    message.sendToTarget();
  }
}
```

When the thread starts, we read the available data using the `AdkManager` `read` method. This method returns an `AdkMessage` instance that contains the raw received bytes and some utilities to parse the response; in our case, we use the `getByte` method to get the first received byte. As the last step, we should publish the collected value through the main thread handler. We then create a `Message` instance using the `obtainMessage` method, which will pull a new message from the handler messages pool. Now we can dispatch the message to the main thread using the `sendToTarget` method.

6. Add the `DataReader` `start()` method to start a scheduler that spawns threads periodically:

```
public void start() {
  // Initialize threads
  SensorThread thread = new SensorThread();
  // Should start over and over publishing results

  Executors.newSingleThreadScheduledExecutor();
  mScheduler.scheduleAtFixedRate(thread, 0,
  HEARTBEAT_POLLING, TimeUnit.MILLISECONDS);
}
```

When we call this method from the `Monitor` activity, the `ExecutorService` parameter will be initialized using the `newSingleThreadScheduledExecutor()` function. This will create a single-threaded executor that guarantees to execute no more than one task at any given time despite the polling period. As the last step, we use a periodical scheduler to run our `SensorThread` every `HEARTBEAT_POLLING` milliseconds.

7. Add the `stop()` method to the `DataReader` class to stop the schedule from spawning new threads. In our case, we simply use the `shutdown()` executor's method:

```
public void stop() {
  // Should stop the calling function
mScheduler.shutdown();
}
```

8. Now we should go back to the `Monitor` class to start and stop our thread scheduler within the activity lifecycle. Add the `DataReader` declaration at the top of the `Monitor` class:

```
private AdkManager mAdkManager;
private DataReader mReader;
```

9. Start and stop the reading scheduler in the `onResume()` and `onPause()` activity's callbacks, as you can see in the following highlighted code:

```
@Override
protected void onResume() {
  super.onResume();
  mAdkManager.open();
  mReader = new DataReader(mAdkManager, this);
  mReader.start();
}
```

```
@Override
protected void onPause() {
 super.onPause();
 mReader.stop();
 mAdkManager.close();
}
```

There is nothing left to do and our prototype is ready to be deployed. Now we can put our index finger between the photoresistor and the LED and take a look at the Android application while the result is updated each 10 seconds.

Enhancing the prototype

Even if the prototype obtains good results, we may want more accurate readings. A great enhancement for the physical application can be reached with a better housing for the photoresistor and the bright LED. Indeed, if we can remove the environment light and make both components more stable during readings, we can have great improvements.

A good approach to achieve this goal is to use an easy-to-get component: *a wooden peg*. We can drill the peg in one go, so the holes are lined up. In this way, we can put the photoresistor in one hole while the LED is in the other one. The rest of components and the breadboard itself remain unaltered. The following illustration shows a wooden peg to house both the components:

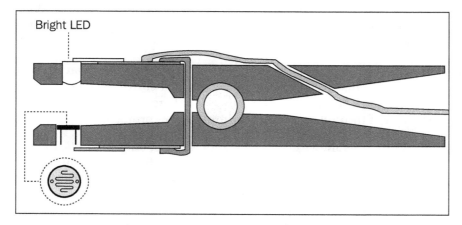

Another improvement is to change and play with the algorithm parameters available in the sketch. Changing the interval and the samples number may obtain better results; however, we have to keep in mind that these changes may also get worse readings. The following is a collection of algorithm parameters that we may change:

```
#define SAMPLES 10
#define POS_THRESHOLD 3
#define NEG_THRESHOLD -3
#define HEARTBEAT_POLL_PERIOD 50
#define SECONDS 10
```

For instance, if we find that our photoresistor works badly with 50 milliseconds of the `HEARTBEAT_POLL_PERIOD` object-like macro, we may try to use more common timings such as 100 or 200 milliseconds.

Summary

In this chapter, we explored the use of external sensors to improve the capabilities of our physical applications. We discovered how a sensor works and we took a look at an example that detects distance and object proximity.

As the first step, we got some information about the biological process of the heartbeat and we found how a photoresistor together with a bright LED could help us to detect the heart rate. We did some initial experiments using our first heart monitor prototype and collected various absolute values that we plotted later into a chart. After the first analysis, we saw that each peak could be a heartbeat and this brought us to enhance the reading phase with an algorithm capable of computing differences between readings during chosen intervals.

With the previous values, we plotted a new chart and discovered that we should check when there is a phase change to find a possible heartbeat. Indeed, our last work was to add a function to calculate the heart rate ready to be sent back to the Android application through the ADK communication protocol.

To show the previous result, we created a layout for our Android application. We configured and used the ADKToolkit library to simplify the communication process. Through a `ScheduledExecutorService` instance, that launches short-lived threads for data collection, we set the processed heart rate in a custom user interface. At the end of this chapter, we explored how to improve our working prototype with some advice that we can follow before proceeding with the next chapter.

In the next chapter, we will build another physical application that uses an external component to control the Android application. It will make use of some Android native APIs to realize, in an easy way, some features that will not be possible without an over complicated hardware and sketch.

Managing Interactions with Physical Components

5

Electronic devices have changed our life. We are surrounded by quite a few invisible objects that collect and eventually compute environment data. Like we saw in the previous chapter, these devices use sensors to retrieve information and we can find them in our everyday life, for example, in our car, when we're walking through supermarkets' sliding doors, and maybe when we're coming back to home.

We can inspire ourselves looking at these things and build amazing physical applications that are capable of reacting to the environment and, indirectly, to the people around. However, if our project expects a direct human interaction, we may need to manage this interaction with physical components.

The goal of this chapter is to build a web radio that uses built-in Android APIs to manage Internet streams, while all interactions are managed by physical components, such as in the old fashioned radios.

In this chapter, we will cover the following topics:

- Managing user interactions
- Building a web radio with physical interactions
- Sending multiple data with Arduino
- Writing an Android application for audio streaming

Managing user interactions

One aspect that distinguishes an interactive prototype is the capability to react to any action made by users. As we've seen in the previous chapter, sensors are one of the most important building blocks to achieve this important goal. However, sometimes, we want to provide a physical interaction where users are capable of altering the application's behavior with their hands, despite the presence of sensors. These parts that are still largely diffused, are simple **mechanic** or **electronic** components that convert analog movements into digital values that our microcontroller can use to alter the program flow. There are a lot of components that we may use to interact with our device: **push buttons**, **switch buttons**, **joysticks**, **knobs**, **pedals**, and **levers**, are just examples of these kind of components.

Knobs are components that we can use to alter some prototype configurations. Indeed, we may create a maintenance console that alters some device constants to prevent the recompilation and upload phase of a new sketch. At other times, knobs are used to make direct actions and their usage is an active part of the users interactions. A common use of knobs is related to electrical devices, such as volume controls in audio equipment.

Another example could be related to robot rovers, when we want to provide direct control for users instead of the robot's own artificial intelligence. In this case, we may use a push button that facilitates the stopping action while activating a manual mode. For instance, we could provide a joystick that can be used to pilot the rover movements.

 An example of the usage of push buttons is related to stopping any actions made by the microcontroller or the prototype. This use of push buttons is called **emergency stop** and it's used in many DIY projects when they are fully automated and equipped with moving parts.

All these elements have two base components in common: **switches** and **potentiometers**. Push buttons are good examples of mechanical switches that close or open a circuit and control the current flow through the microcontroller pins. In this way, we may activate a particular functionality of our circuit like we did in *Chapter 3, Testing your Physical Application*, according to the detected voltage.

Potentiometers, instead, are electronic components, more like resistors. The electronic part is composed of three terminal legs that we can use in different ways to change the purpose of the potentiometer. Indeed, if we connect one end and the central leg to a component, it acts as a **variable resistor**. On the other hand, if we use all three terminals, it works like an adjustable **voltage divider**. The *shaft* of a potentiometer that we can turn from one direction to the other, is used to change the value of the resistor or the voltage divider. Good examples of the application of potentiometers are knobs, joysticks, and guitar pedals.

Building a web radio with physical interaction

Microcontrollers aren't designed for complicated work, so we need to be careful to partition the needs of our project to the right environments. For a web radio, we can use the microcontroller to read the knobs and switches, and let the Android APIs and UDOO's powerful CPU do the rest. This will keep Android from getting distracted while reading the hardware, and will prevent the microcontroller from getting overloaded with the complications of network streaming and playback.

The first part of our prototype is to build a circuit and write a sketch that collects values from two potentiometers and a push button:

- We use the first potentiometer to change the active radio station and to increase or decrease the audio volume
- We use the physical button to control the radio playback

In this way, we're removing all interactions done through the Android user interface.

As the first step, grab two potentiometers and connect them to the board so that we can realize the following circuit:

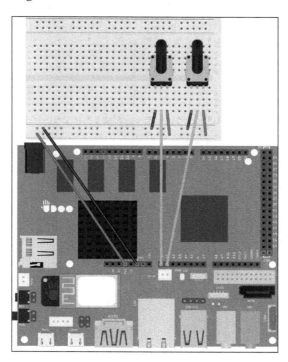

Follow the procedure given below to get the circuit connected to the potentiometer, as shown in the preceding schema:

1. Put two potentiometers on the right of your breadboard, because we need to use the free slots on the left for the push button.

2. Connect the UDOO +3.3V pin to the positive line of the power bus. Be sure not to connect the +5V power pin because it may damage the analog input pins during future connections.

3. Connect the UDOO ground to the negative line of the power bus.

4. Connect the left terminal of the first potentiometer to the negative line of the power bus.

 Potentiometers act like resistors, so there aren't any differences if you connect the wrong positive terminal. The only side effect is that the detected values will not start from a range [0-1023] but from [1023-0]. If you notice that, *invert these connections*.

5. Connect the right terminal of the first potentiometer to the positive line of the power bus.

6. Connect the middle terminal to the analog input A0.

7. Repeat points 4, 5, 6 for the second potentiometer and connect its middle terminal to the analog input A1.

With this circuit, we use both potentiometers as voltage dividers and when we turn the shaft, the microcontroller notices a change in the voltage output and transforms this value in to a numeric range [0-1023]. This circuit is really similar to the one built in the previous chapter to create a light sensor, but since the potentiometer already has a resistor in its package, we don't need any other electric components to keep it working.

Now we need a push button to start and stop the playback. We have to add the component on the left of the breadboard and connect it to UDOO as follows:

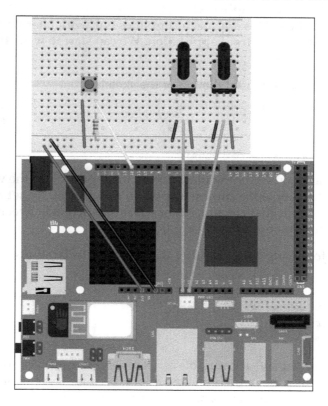

Follow the given steps to connect the components, as shown in the preceding schema:

1. Connect the left terminal of the push button to the positive line of the power bus.

2. Connect the right terminal to the negative line of the power bus using 10 KOhm resistor.

3. Connect the right terminal to pin 12 of the UDOO board.

With this circuit, we can read the value of the push button using pin 12 of the UDOO board; when the button is pressed, we can change an internal state of the microcontroller.

Now that we have a circuit with all the required components, we have to start a new sketch and prepare a function that we can use to collect all data. The goal of the sketch is to prepare a **triple** that has the *playback status*, the *volume* and the *station* as ordered values. This approach simplifies our work later when we start communication with the Android application. We can start to write the new sketch as follows:

1. Define the connections at the top of the sketch:

```
#define RADIO_POLL_PERIOD 100
#define PLAY_BUTTON 12
#define KNOB_VOLUME A0
#define KNOB_TUNER A1
```

   We are using pin 12 for the play button, the input A0 for the volume, and the input A1 to change the current station. In this project, we set a polling time of 100 milliseconds that is required for a fast interaction between our physical components and the Android application.

2. Add the following variables after the previous declarations:

```
boolean playback = true;
int buttonRead = LOW;
int previousRead = LOW;
int tuner = 0;
int volume = 0;
```

   We are using a playback variable as a simple state indicator so that the sketch knows whether the radio is playing or not. Because we're building a radio that relies on physical interactions, it's important that the device state contained in the sketch is considered the *source of truth* for the entire application and that Android should trust these values. We're also defining other variables to store the readings from the button and the two potentiometers.

3. Add the pin mode in the setup() function and open the serial communication:

```
void setup() {
  pinMode(PLAY_BUTTON, INPUT);
  Serial.begin(115200);
}
```

4. Create a `readData()` function at the bottom of the sketch in which we detect the user input from physical components:

```
void readData() {
  buttonRead = digitalRead(PLAY_BUTTON);
  if (buttonRead == HIGH && previousRead != buttonRead) {
    playback = !playback;
  }
  previousRead = buttonRead;
  tuner = analogRead(KNOB_TUNER);
  volume = analogRead(KNOB_VOLUME);
}
```

In the first part, we assign the value of the push button to the `buttonRead` variable to check whether it's pressed or not. We also store in the `previousRead` variable the last detected value because we want to avoid wrong state changes during continuous readings. In this way, if a user holds the button, only one state change occurs.

In the last lines, we make `analogRead` calls to collect data from both the potentiometers.

5. Call the `readData()` function inside the main `loop()` function and print the collected values as follows:

```
void loop() {
  readData();
  Serial.print("Playing music: ");
  Serial.println(playback);
  Serial.print("Radio station: ");
  Serial.println(tuner);
  Serial.print("Volume: ");
  Serial.println(volume);
  delay(RADIO_POLL_PERIOD);
}
```

Now we can upload the sketch into our board and open the **serial monitor** to start playing with knobs and the playback button. The following is an example of an expected output:

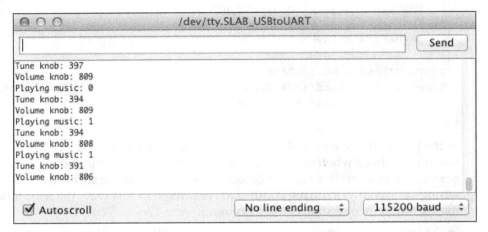

Normalizing collected data before sending

As we noticed, if we turn the potentiometers shafts or if we push the playback button, our values change immediately. This is a really good starting point, but now we have to transform these data so that they can be easily used by the Android application.

Because we want to manage five radio stations, the sketch should map the tuner readings into values between the range [0-4]. We are going to create fixed intervals in the [0-1023] range, so when we turn the shaft and pass one interval, the active station should be updated. To implement this mapping, we have to follow these steps:

1. At the top of the sketch, add the highlighted declarations:

   ```
   #define KNOB_TUNER A1
   #define STATIONS 5
   #define MAX_ANALOG_READ 1024.0
   const float tunerInterval = MAX_ANALOG_READ / STATIONS;
   boolean playback = true;
   ```

   We define the number of managed stations as 5 and we set the maximum analog read value. In this way, we can reuse the above object-like macros to define the `tunerInterval` constant to map readings into the right interval.

2. Add the `mapStations()` function at the bottom of the sketch:

```
int mapStations(int analogValue) {
    int currentStation = analogValue / tunerInterval;
}
```

To find the `currentStation` variable, we divide the analog reading with the tuner interval. In this way, we're sure that returned value is bounded to [0-4] range.

Using the preceding map function is not sufficient to let our radio work. Another required step is to convert the volume value because Android uses a float number in the range [0.0-1.0]. For this reason, we should normalize the volume knob through the following steps:

1. Add this function below the `mapStations()` function:

```
float normalizeVolume(int analogValue) {
    return analogValue / MAX_ANALOG_READ;
}
```

2. Change the main `loop()` function as follows so that we can check whether all the values are transformed correctly:

```
void loop() {
    readData();
    Serial.print("Playing music: ");
    Serial.println(playback);
    Serial.print("Radio station: ");
    Serial.println(mapStations(tuner));
    Serial.print("Volume: ");
    Serial.println(normalizeVolume(volume));
    delay(RADIO_POLL_PERIOD);
}
```

3. Upload the new sketch to see the results shown in the following screenshot:

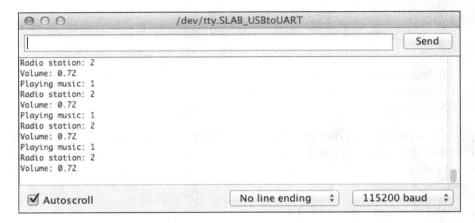

 Through the preceding steps, we collected data from the physical input devices and transformed these values to calculate the current station and radio volume from knobs. However, we need to put this logic even in our Android application because it should map for each possible station, the related URL of web streaming. This means that the same logic is replicated and this isn't a good approach, especially if we need to add new channels in the future. In this case, our code must be changed in both applications, and we should always avoid the situations that are *error prone*. A good approach is to use the microcontroller only for input reporting and let the Android application manage and transform received raw data. We use this approach only for the scope of the book to help you get more comfortable with the sketch code.

Sending multiple data with Arduino

In *Chapter 4, Using Sensors to Listen to the Environment*, we needed to send a single byte computed by the microcontroller. However, in most common cases, we need to read data from different sensors or physical components and we may need to send them back to Android at once. In this prototype, we should observe this requirement because the microcontroller must read all three values and send them back with only one ADK write. A simple approach is to build a string that represents our triple, and uses the comma to separate these values with the format `<playback>,<volume>,<station>`. Through this representation, we obtain the following values :

```
0,0.332768,2
1,0.951197,4
```

Then we can write the *serialized* representation of the radio state in the ADK buffer and proceed with the *deserialization* in the Android application.

 We may think about implementing or using a more complex communication protocol to transfer generic data from Arduino to Android, but we should always bear in mind that, at the beginning, every good idea must follow the **KISS principle: Keep It Simple, Stupid** (a design principle noted by the U.S. Navy in 1960). Because the more simple the software, the more likely it is to work well.

We need to write the accessory descriptor at the top of the sketch, like the following proposed code snippet:

```
#include <adk.h>
#define BUFFSIZE 128
char accessoryName[] = "Web radio";
char manufacturer[] = "Example, Inc.";
char model[] = "WebRadio";
char versionNumber[] = "0.1.0";
char serialNumber[] = "1";
char url[] = "http://www.example.com";
uint8_t buffer[BUFFSIZE];
USBHost Usb;
ADK adk(&Usb, manufacturer, model, accessoryName, versionNumber,
url, serialNumber);
```

We also need a second buffer that will hold the triple; we can add its declaration just before the ADK buffer variable as follows:

```
char triple[BUFFSIZE];
uint8_t buffer[BUFFSIZE];
```

At the bottom of the sketch, add the following function to write the triple in the ADK buffer:

```
void writeBuffer(int playback, float volume, int station) {
    sprintf(triple, "%f,%f,%f", (float) playback,
      normalizeVolume(volume), (float) mapStations(station));
    memcpy(buffer, triple, BUFFSIZE);
}
```

The `writeBuffer()` function expects three parameters used in triple building. To achieve this, we use the `sprintf()` function to write these values in the intermediate `triple` buffer. In the `sprintf()` function call, we also use the `normalizeVolume()` and `mapStations()` functions to get the transformed values. We then use the `memcpy()` function to write the `triple` variable in the ADK `buffer`.

We need this extra step because we cannot write the `triple` variable in the ADK `buffer`. The `adk.write()` function expects an `unsigned char*` type while the triple is a `char*` type.

Now that the ADK buffer contains the serialized data, we have to remove all `Serial` calls and rewrite the main `loop()` function as follows:

```
void loop() {
  Usb.Task();
  if (adk.isReady()) {
    readData();
    writeBuffer(playback, volume, tuner);
    adk.write(BUFFSIZE, buffer);
  }
  delay(RADIO_POLL_PERIOD);
}
```

When the ADK is ready, we read data from the push button and both potentiometers, and then we serialize these values in a triple that will be written in the ADK output buffer. When everything is ready, we send the recorded input back to Android.

We can now update our sketch and complete the prototype with the Android application.

Streaming audio from Android applications

The Android operating system provides a great collection of UI components, an important building block for all physical applications. All of them are specific for phone or tablet interaction and this is an outstanding improvement because users already know how to use them. However, Android isn't just a collection of UI components because it allows many APIs to achieve recurring tasks. In our case, we want a physical application that is capable of interacting with a web service to open and reproduce an audio stream.

Without the i.MX6 processor and the Android operating system, this task will never be easy to implement, but in our case, UDOO board provides all that we need.

Designing the Android user interface

From Android Studio, start a new application called **WebRadio** with **Android API 19**. During the bootstrap process, choose a **Blank Activity** named **Radio**.

Our first goal is to change the default layout in favor of a simple but fancy interface. The main layout must show the current activated radio station providing different information such as an optional image – the name of the channel together with a description. Before writing down the XML code required by Android to draw the user interface, we should plan our work to detect the required components. In the following screenshot, we can take a look at the user interface mock-up that provides all the required elements:

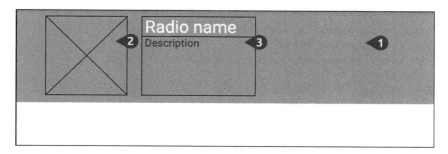

The above layout includes a number marker that defines in which order the components will be created. According to this layout, we should provide three different views in the following order:

1. As the first step, we should create a background frame with a different color to provide a block in which we will put all other components.

2. Even if this is optional, we can prepare a box that will host the radio channel image, if it's available.

3. The last block includes two different text areas where the first represents the channel name, while the other represents the channel description.

With this layout design, we should proceed and replace the standard theme with the following steps:

1. In the `res/values/dimens.xml` resource file, add the following definitions to provide some dimensions for our components, such as the background frame height and the font size:

    ```
    <resources>
      <dimen name="activity_horizontal_margin">16dp</dimen>
      <dimen name="activity_vertical_margin">16dp</dimen>
      <dimen name="activity_frame_height">220dp</dimen>
      <dimen name="activity_image_square">180dp</dimen>
    ```

```
<dimen name="layout_padding">50dp</dimen>
<dimen name="title_size">40sp</dimen>
<dimen name="description_size">25sp</dimen>
</resources>
```

2. In the `res/values/styles.xml` resource file, add the following colors used by the background frame and text elements:

```
<resources>
  <color name="picton_blue">#33B5E5</color>
  <color name="white">#FFFFFF</color>
  <style name="AppTheme"
    parent="Theme.AppCompat.Light.DarkActionBar">
  </style>
</resources>
```

3. In the `activity_radio.xml` file under `res/layout/`, replace the `RelativeLayout` with the following `FrameLayout` to implement the background frame:

```
<FrameLayout xmlns:android="http://schemas.android.com/apk/res/
android"
  xmlns:tools="http://schemas.android.com/tools"
  android:layout_width="match_parent"
  android:layout_height="@dimen/activity_frame_height"
  android:paddingLeft="@dimen/activity_horizontal_margin"
  android:paddingRight="@dimen/activity_horizontal_margin"
  android:paddingTop="@dimen/activity_vertical_margin"
  android:paddingBottom="@dimen/activity_vertical_margin"
  android:background="@color/picton_blue"
  tools:context=".Radio">
</FrameLayout>
```

We use the `FrameLayout` to create a section that houses all other components with the defined height and background color.

4. Create a `LinearLayout` nested in the above `FrameLayout` parameter:

```
<LinearLayout
  android:orientation="horizontal"
  android:layout_width="match_parent"
  android:layout_height="match_parent">

  <ImageView
    android:id="@+id/radio_image"
    android:src="@drawable/ic_launcher"
    android:layout_height="@dimen/activity_image_square"
```

```
    android:layout_width=
      "@dimen/activity_image_square" />

  <LinearLayout
    android:orientation="vertical"
    android:layout_marginLeft="@dimen/layout_padding"
    android:layout_width="match_parent"
    android:layout_height="match_parent">
  </LinearLayout>
</LinearLayout>
```

The first `LinearLayout` will contain the `radio_image ImageView` that changes according to the active channel. The second `LinearLayout` is used to host the radio name and description.

5. Add within the second `LinearLayout` the following views:

```
<TextView
  android:id="@+id/radio_name"
  android:text="Radio name"
  android:textColor="@color/white"
  android:textSize="@dimen/title_size"
  android:layout_width="wrap_content"
  android:layout_height="wrap_content" />

<TextView
  android:id="@+id/radio_description"
  android:text="Description"
  android:textSize="@dimen/description_size"
  android:layout_width="wrap_content"
  android:layout_height="wrap_content" />
```

According to previous defined styles, the following is the obtained layout:

Before we can proceed with the logic implementation, we have to get all view references during the `onCreate()` callback through the following steps:

1. Add the following declarations at the top of the `Radio` class:

   ```
   private TextView mRadioName;
   private TextView mRadioDescription;
   private ImageView mRadioImage;
   ```

2. At the bottom of the `onCreate()` callback, add the highlighted code:

   ```
   setContentView(R.layout.activity_radio);
   mRadioName = (TextView) findViewById(R.id.radio_name);
   mRadioDescription = (TextView)
   findViewById(R.id.radio_description);
   mRadioImage = (ImageView) findViewById(R.id.radio_image);
   ```

Now that the layout is completed, we can proceed with the ADK configuration.

Setting up the ADK Toolkit

Before we begin the web radio implementation, we should first configure the *ADKToolkit* like we did in the previous chapter. To have a working ADK configuration, follow these steps:

1. Add the *ADKToolkit* library dependency in the `build.gradle` file under `app`.

2. Sync your Gradle configuration.

3. Create the accessory filter file `usb_accessory_filter.xml` under `res/xml/` using the following code:

   ```
   <resources>
     <usb-accessory
       version="0.1.0"
       model="WebRadio"
       manufacturer="Example, Inc."/>
   </resources>
   ```

4. Add the *USB accessory support* option requirement and the *USB accessory intent filter* option in the `AndroidManifest.xml` file.

5. In the `Radio.java` class file, declare the `AdkManager` object at the top of the class.

6. Add the `AdkManager` initialization inside the `onCreate` method of the `Radio` activity class.

7. Override the `onPause()` and `onResume()` callbacks to start and stop the ADK connection according to the activity lifecycle.

 The above checklist should be used every time we start a new project. It's a good idea to write down these steps and be sure that our projects always start with this ADK configuration.

8. As a last step of the initial configuration, we need to add the Internet access permission because we are going to use network streams. Add in the following permission inside the tag manifest in your `AndroidManifest.xml` file:

```
<uses-permission android:name="android.permission.INTERNET"
/>
```

Changing web radio stations

The next step is to write the required Android code to play and stop configured radio stations. What we need is to formalize the station object and a utility class that abstracts the same functionalities of the built-in media player. The following is the checklist of required classes with their usage:

- `Station`: Formalizes the audio channel and includes the title, the description, and the station image, together with the streaming URL required to start the remote playback

- `RadioManager`: Configures all available stations during its initialization and abstracts all common methods to manage the playback and the channel switching

We begin with the `Station` class that we can realize with the following steps:

1. Create a new Java package inside our namespace called `streaming`.

2. Create the `Station` class in the newly created Java package and add the following declarations and class constructor:

```
private final static String STREAMING_BASE_URL =
"https://streaming.jamendo.com/";
private String title;
private String description;
private int imageId;
public Station(String title, String description, int
imageId) {
  this.title = title;
  this.description = description;
  this.imageId = imageId;
}
```

We define the first part of the URL that we will use to construct the channel streaming URL. In this case, we are going to use the **Jamendo** service that offers many music channels that are released under the **Creative Commons** license. If you want to get more information, you can take a look at the service website:

```
https://www.jamendo.com
```

Other attributes that we will use are the station `title` and `description` attributes and the Android resource identifier.

3. At the bottom of the class, the following getters are used to retrieve instance attributes:

```java
public String getTitle() {
  return title;
}
public String getDescription() {
  return description;
}
public int getImageId() {
  return imageId;
}
public String getStreamUrl() {
  return STREAMING_BASE_URL + title;
}
```

In the `getStreamUrl()` method, we are using the base URL with the radio name to find the correct audio stream.

 This string concatenation is related to how the Jamendo service works. If you use another service or you don't want to use the title attribute during the URL composition, you should change this method.

Now that we have a formal `Station` class representation, we need to define the class capable of managing the Android playback. We realize the `RadioManager` class through the following steps:

1. In the `streaming` package, create the `RadioManager` class and add the following declarations at the beginning:

```java
private static ArrayList<Station> mChannels;
private static MediaPlayer mMediaPlayer;
private static int mPlayback;
private static int mIndex;
private static Station mActiveStation;
```

We use the Android high-level MediaPlayer object to manage remote streaming; we make use of some status variables, such as the current active station with its array index and the playback status. We will fill the mChannels ArrayList object during the RadioManager class initialization and it will host all the available music channels.

2. Add the initializer method at the bottom of the class, as follows:

```
public static void initialize() {
  // Prepare all stations object
  mChannels = new ArrayList();
  mChannels.add(new Station("JamPop", "Pop",
  R.drawable.ic_launcher));
  mChannels.add(new Station("JamClassical", "Classical",
  R.drawable.ic_launcher));
  mChannels.add(new Station("JamJazz", "Jazz",
  R.drawable.ic_launcher));
  mChannels.add(new Station("JamElectro", "Electronic",
  R.drawable.ic_launcher));
  mChannels.add(new Station("JamRock", "Rock",
  R.drawable.ic_launcher));
  // Initializes the MediaPlayer with listeners
  mMediaPlayer = new MediaPlayer();
  mMediaPlayer.setAudioStreamType
  (AudioManager.STREAM_MUSIC);
  mMediaPlayer.setOnPreparedListener(new MediaPlayer.
  OnPreparedListener() {
    @Override
    public void onPrepared(MediaPlayer mediaPlayer) {
      mediaPlayer.start();
    }
  });
}
```

In the first part, we configure the list of all the available stations according to the previous Station constructor. We configure the MediaPlayer object so that it starts a network stream immediately when the prepare process is completed.

You can find more information about how the Android MediaPlayer class works at the URL:

http://developer.android.com/reference/android/ media/MediaPlayer.html.

3. Add the following methods to abstract the play and stop functionalities to prevent code repeating:

```
private static void stop() {
  mMediaPlayer.reset();
}
private static void play() {
  try {
    mMediaPlayer.setDataSource
    (mActiveStation.getStreamUrl());
    mMediaPlayer.prepareAsync();
  }
  catch (IOException e) {
    // noop
  }
}
```

When the player is stopped, we have to reset the media player object because we may need to set another data source immediately. The `play` method sets the streaming URL of the current activated station and starts a nonblocking prepare task.

4. Add the following public method that changes the playback status:

```
public static void playback(int value) {
  // If the playback status has changed
  if (value != mPlayback) {
    // Play or stop the playback
    if (value == 0) {
      stop();
    }
    else {
      play();
    }
    mPlayback = value;
  }
}
```

The sketch through the ADK sends continuous data to our application every 100 milliseconds and this enhances the responsiveness of the user interface. However, we don't want to repeat the same command many times, so we only do something if the value received is different from the stored one. In the second part, we choose to start or play the current stream according to the given parameter.

5. As the last part, we need a method to change the activated channel. Add the following code at the bottom of the class:

```
public static Station changeStation(int stationId) {
  Station station = null;
  if (stationId != mIndex) {
    mIndex = stationId;
    // Set the current station
    mActiveStation = mChannels.get(mIndex);
    station = mActiveStation;
    stop();
    if (mPlayback == 1) {
      play();
    }
  }
  return station;
}
```

As we did earlier, we avoid changing the station if the received value is the same as the one we currently played. Then, we update the current channel and stop the last stream. In this way, if we are in the playback state, we can safely reproduce a new station stream. In any case, we return the chosen Station instance, or null if the station has not changed.

Reading input from physical devices

Like we did in the previous chapter, we need to prepare our application to make continuous readings of user input available in the ADK buffer. As we did before, we are going to create a Java interface that exposes the required methods to update the user interface. We can achieve this through the following steps:

1. Create a new Java interface called OnDataChanges and add the following method:

```
public interface OnDataChanges {
  void updateStation(Station station);
}
```

2. Let the Radio class implement the preceding interface through the highlighted code:

```
public class Radio extends ActionBarActivity implements
OnDataChanges {
```

3. Implement the interface code at the end of the class to update the Android user interface:

```
@Override
public void updateStation(Station station) {
  mRadioName.setText(station.getTitle());
  mRadioDescription.setText(station.getDescription());
  mRadioImage.setImageResource(station.getImageId());
}
```

In this part, we simply update all views according to the `station` instance attributes.

The last required step is to implement our scheduled thread that reads processed data from the microcontroller and updates the `MediaPlayer` class streaming together with the Android user interface. To complete this last building block, perform the following steps:

1. Create a new package in your namespace called `adk`.

2. In the `adk` package, add a new class named `DataReader`.

3. At the top of the class, add the following declarations:

```
private final static int INPUT_POLLING = 100;
private final static int STATION_UPDATE = 0;
private AdkManager mAdkManager;
private OnDataChanges mCaller;
private ScheduledExecutorService mScheduler;
private Handler mMainLoop;
```

Like we did in the previous chapter, we're defining the polling time and the message type used by the main thread handler. We also store the references for the `AdkManager` parameter and the caller activity to use, respectively, the ADK read method and the `updateStation` function's callback. Then we define the `ExecutorService` method implementation together with the main thread `Handler`.

4. Implement the `DataReader` constructor to set the message handler when the main thread receives a new message from the background thread:

```
public DataReader(AdkManager adkManager, OnDataChanges caller) {
  this.mAdkManager = adkManager;
  this.mCaller = caller;
  mMainLoop = new Handler(Looper.getMainLooper()) {
    @Override
    public void handleMessage(Message message) {
      switch (message.what) {
```

```
    case STATION_UPDATE:
      mCaller.updateStation((Station) message.obj);
      break;
    }
  }
};
}
```

We store the `AdkManager` and the `caller` activity references and then set
a `Handler` attached to the application's main looper. The `handleMessage`
callback checks the message code to identify the `STATION_UPDATE` messages.
In this case, we call the `updateStation` method and pass the attached object.

5. At the bottom of `DataReader` class, add the following private class that
   implements the `Runnable` interface to read and manage the physical
   input devices:

```
private class InputThread implements Runnable {
  @Override
  public void run() {
    // Read from ADK
    AdkMessage response = mAdkManager.read();
    // Parse the response
    String[] collectedInputs =
    response.getString().split(",");
    int playback = (int)
    Float.parseFloat(collectedInputs[0]);
    int station = (int)
    Float.parseFloat(collectedInputs[2]);
    // Start radio and get the changed station
    RadioManager.playback(playback);
    Station currentStation =
    RadioManager.changeStation(station);
    // Updated station back to the main thread
    if (currentStation != null) {
      Message message = mMainLoop.obtainMessage
      (STATION_UPDATE, currentStation);
      message.sendToTarget();
    }
  }
}
```

When the thread starts, we read user inputs using the `AdkManager` method. Then we get the raw string from the response and use the split method to deserialize the received triple. The first position refers to the playback status and we use it in the `RadioManager` class to start or stop the playback. The value in the third position is the activated channel and we pass this to the `changeStation` method. According to the previous implementation, if the `currentStation` variable is not changed, we avoid publishing the message to the main thread to prevent useless interface redraws.

6. Add a method to the `DataReader` class to start the scheduler that spawns short-lived threads periodically:

```
public void start() {
  // Initialize threads
  InputThread thread = new InputThread();
  // Should start over and over while publishing results
  mScheduler = Executors.
  newSingleThreadScheduledExecutor();
  mScheduler.scheduleAtFixedRate(thread, 0, INPUT_POLLING,
  TimeUnit.MILLISECONDS);
}
```

Like we did in the previous project, we use a scheduler that spawns a single `InputThread` parameter every time at a `INPUT_POLLING` variable milliseconds.

7. Add the stop method at the bottom of the class to stop the scheduler from spawning new threads through the `shutdown` executor's method:

```
public void stop() {
  mScheduler.shutdown();
}
```

8. Now we should go back to the `Radio` class to start and stop the scheduler within the activity lifecycle. Add the `DataReader` method declaration at the top of the `Radio` class:

```
private AdkManager mAdkManager;
private DataReader mReader;
```

9. Initialize the `RadioManager` class and the `DataReader` instance when the activity is created through the following highlighted code, that you should add at the bottom of the `onCreate()` callback:

```
mRadioImage = (ImageView) findViewById(R.id.radio_image);
RadioManager.initialize();
mAdkManager = new AdkManager(this);
mReader = new DataReader(mAdkManager, this);
```

10. Start and stop the reading scheduler in the `onResume()` and `onPause()` activity's callbacks as you can see in the highlighted code:

```
@Override
protected void onPause() {
  super.onPause();
  mReader.stop();
  mAdkManager.close();
}

@Override
protected void onResume() {
  super.onResume();
  mAdkManager.open();
  mReader.start();
}
```

With these last steps, the radio station is completed and we can upload the Android application in the UDOO board and start playing with the station knob and the push button.

 Because we didn't manage network errors, be sure that UDOO is connected to the Internet and that you're using the Ethernet or the Wi-Fi network adapter, otherwise the application will not work.

Managing audio volume

Before we can release our first radio prototype, we should manage the volume knob from the Android application. This part is really easy thanks to the `MediaPlayer` method APIs, because it exposes a public method to change the volume of the activated stream. To improve our project with a volume manager, we need to add the following code snippets:

1. In the `RadioManager` class, add the highlighted declaration at the top of the class:

```
private static Station mActiveStation;
private static float mVolume = 1.0f;
```

2. At the bottom of the `RadioManager` class, add this public method:

```
public static void setVolume(float volume) {
  if (Math.abs(mVolume - volume) > 0.05) {
    mVolume = volume;
    mMediaPlayer.setVolume(volume, volume);
  }
}
```

The method `setVolume` expects the float received from Arduino as argument and we use it to change the volume of the `mMediaPlayer` instance. However, because we don't want to change the volume for little variations, we discard all requests for values that aren't so different from the previous recorded input.

3. Add the volume parsing and the `setVolume` function call within the `InputThread` implementation that we wrote in the `DataReader` class:

```
float volume = Float.parseFloat(collectedInputs[1]);
int station = (int) Float.parseFloat(collectedInputs [2]);
RadioManager.playback(playback);
RadioManager.setVolume(volume);
```

With this last piece, the web radio is completed and we can proceed with this last deployment. Now our users can interact and enjoy the prototype using both knobs and the push button to control every aspect of the application.

Improving the prototype

Before we go further with other prototypes, we should think about how we can improve our devices when some unexpected events occur. A good starting point is to think about error handling and, in particular, what happens if the Android application stops hearing incoming data from the accessory. There are many approaches to prevent wrong actions and a good solution is to include a default behavior in the Android application that the prototype should follow in these emergency cases.

We could have used another periodic timer that increases a variable every time it gets executed. When the `InputThread` instance completes a successful reading, it should reset the above variable. In this way, we can monitor for how much time we stop receiving user inputs and according to this time, we may decide to change the application's behavior. Through this variable, for example, we could stop the radio playback, or turn down the volume a little bit if the accessory stops providing user inputs.

The key point is that we should always design our prototype both for failure and success. Most *what happens if* problems are easy to incorporate up front, but hard to add in later.

Summary

In this chapter, you learned how to improve the quality of our prototypes when human interaction is required. We explored some of the common physical components that can be used to alter or control Android applications. Through powerful Android APIs, we built a web radio capable of complex tasks like network streaming.

In the first part, we built the required circuit using two potentiometers and a push button. When we checked returned values through the serial monitor, we saw that they are not so useful in this format, so we wrote a mapping and a normalization functions.

We continued providing a new layout for the Android application, but we avoided adding any kind of interaction through the user interface. We wrote a class to abstract all possible interactions with the built-in media player, so that we can easily control this component in any part of our application. Indeed, we used it within the background task, and every time it read user inputs, it immediately changed the state of the radio. In this way, we enabled the push button to start and stop the playback and the two potentiometers to change the active station and the music volume.

In the next chapter, we start talking about home automation. We start from scratch a new prototype capable of turning on and off external devices using a combination of sensor values and users settings. We will make use of other Android APIs to store the application's settings and use them later to alter the sketch flow.

6
Building a Chronotherm for Home Automation

For many decades now it has been possible, even easy, to control home devices such as lights, thermostats, and appliances with automatic and remote controls. On the one hand, these automation devices save effort and energy, but on the other hand, even modest adjustments are inconvenient to final users because they need a good knowledge of the system to make any changes.

During the last few years, people were reluctant to adopt **home automation** technologies because of a lack of a standard or an easy-to-customize solution. Nowadays, things are changing and prototyping boards such as UDOO, play a great role during the design and the building of **DIY (Do It Yourself)** automated devices. Best of all, thanks to open source projects, these platforms are easy to extend and can be controlled by different devices, such as personal computers with web browsers, mobile phones, and tablets.

In this chapter, we will cover the following topics:

- Exploring the advantages of home automation
- Building a chronotherm circuit
- Sending data and receiving commands
- Writing the Chronotherm Android application

Home automation

The term *home automation* is quite generic and may have a lot of different meanings: a timer controlling ambient lights, an intelligent system that takes actions in response to events coming from the outside, or a programmable device responsible for accomplishing repetitive tasks.

These are all valid examples of home automation as they share the same key concept making us able to manage house work and activities even when we are not at home. Home-automated devices usually operate on public or private networks to communicate with each other, as well as with other kinds of devices such as smartphones or tablets, taking commands or exchanging information about their status. But what happens when we need to automate simple appliances or electronic components such as light bulbs? A common solution to address this problem is by developing a sort of **Control System** device, physically connected to the appliances we want to manage; being the Control System, a home-automated device, we can use it to drive the behavior of every appliance it is connected to.

If we manage to get enough experience in the home-automation field, the chances are that we will be able to develop and build a high-end system for our own house, flexible enough to be easily extended without any further knowledge.

Building a chronotherm circuit

A chronotherm is mainly composed of a *Control Unit,* that has the responsibility to check whether the environment temperature is below a preconfigured setpoint, and in this case, turn on the boiler to warm up the room. This behavior is quite simple, but without any further logic isn't so useful. Indeed, we can extend this behavior adding the *time* parameter to the chronotherm logic. In this way, users can define a temperature setpoint for each hour of the day, making the temperature check smarter.

> The fact that in this prototype the Control Unit is the onboard Arduino is an implementation detail to simplify the overall design.

This is how a traditional chronotherm works and to realize it, we should:

- Build the circuit with a temperature sensor
- Implement the microcontroller logic to check the users' setpoints with the current temperature

Unfortunately, the second part is not so easy because the users' setpoints should be stored in the microcontroller, and for this reason, we can delegate this task to our Android application saving settings in the microSD card. This approach decouples responsibilities in the following way:

- Arduino sketch:
    - Collects data from a temperature sensor
    - Sends the detected temperature to Android
    - Expects an Android command to start or stop the boiler
- Android application:
    - Manages user's interactions
    - Implements user's settings to store temperature setpoints for each hour of the day
    - Reads the temperature sent by the microcontroller
    - Implements the logic to choose whether the boiler should be turned on or off
    - Sends a command to the microcontroller to start or stop the boiler

With this plan, we can rely on the Android user interface components to easily implement a lean and usable interface, while avoiding the complexity of the settings storage layer.

To start building the prototype, we need to plug into our breadboard a temperature sensor, such as the *TMP36*, to obtain the following circuit:

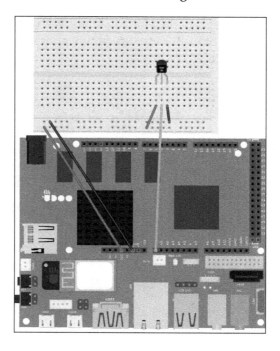

The following is a step-wise procedure to get the components connected, as shown in the preceding schema:

1. Put the TMP36 sensor on the right part of the breadboard.

2. Connect the UDOO +3.3V pin to the positive line of the power bus. Be sure not to connect the +5V power pin because it may damage the analog input pins during future connections.

3. Connect the UDOO ground to the negative line of the power bus.

4. Connect the left terminal of the TMP36 sensor to the positive line of the power bus.

> When using packaged sensors, we can deduce the orientation looking at the flat part. Use this approach to find the left and the right terminal.

5. Connect the right terminal of the TMP36 sensor to the negative line of the power bus.

6. Connect the middle terminal of the TMP36 sensor to the analog input A0.

This packaged sensor is really simple to use and it doesn't require any other components or voltage dividers to provide the voltage variation to the microcontroller. Now we should proceed managing the boiler ignition from our circuit. For the sake of the prototype, we're going to replace the boiler actuator with a simple LED, like we did in *Chapter 2, Know your Tools*. This will keep our circuit simpler.

We can add an LED to the breadboard to achieve the following schema:

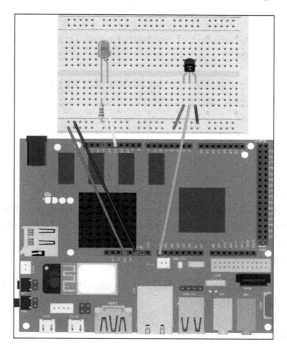

The following is the procedure of connecting the components, as shown in the preceding schema:

1. Put the LED on the left-hand side of the breadboard.
2. Connect the LED longer terminal (anode) to the UDOO digital pin 12.
3. Connect the LED smaller terminal (cathode) to the negative line of the power bus, using a 220 Ohm resistor.

With this circuit, we have all the components required to collect data from the environment and to simulate a boiler ignition. Now we need to open the Arduino IDE and start a new sketch. The first goal is to retrieve and convert the detected temperature into a convenient unit of measurement. To achieve this goal, we have to perform the following steps:

1. Define these object-like macros and variables at the top of the sketch:

    ```
    #define TEMPERATURE_POLL_PERIOD 1000
    #define SENSOR A0
    #define BOILER 12
    int reading;
    ```

    We define the SENSOR object to represent the analog pin A0 while the BOILER object is related to our digital pin 12. We also declare a reading variable that we use later to store the current detected temperature. The TEMPERATURE_ POLL_PERIOD macro represents how many seconds the microcontroller waits between readings and before it notifies the Android application with the detected temperature.

2. In the setup() function, add the pin mode declaration and open the serial communication as follows:

    ```
    void setup() {
      pinMode(BOILER, OUTPUT);
      digitalWrite(BOILER, LOW);
      Serial.begin(115200);
    }
    ```

3. In the bottom of the sketch, create the convertToCelsius() function as follows:

    ```
    float convertToCelsius(int value) {
      float voltage = (value / 1024.0) * 3.3;
      return (voltage - 0.5) * 100;
    }
    ```

In this function, we expect a sensor reading and return its representation in *Celsius degrees*. To achieve this, we're using a little math to figure out what the real detected voltage is. Because the analog to digital converters of the UDOO microcontroller provide values in the range [0-1023], but we want to calculate the range from 0 to 3.3V, we should divide the value by 1024.0 and then multiply the result by 3.3.

We use the voltage in the Celsius conversion because if we read the TMP36 datasheet, we find that every 10 millivolts of change from the sensor is equivalent to a temperature change of 1 Celsius degree and this is why we multiply the value by 100. We also need to subtract the voltage by 0.5 because this sensor handles temperatures below 0 degrees, and 0.5 is the chosen offset.

 This function easily converts TMP36 readings into Celsius degrees. If you want to use another unit of measurement, such as Fahrenheit, or if you use a different sensor or thermistor, you have to change this implementation.

4. In the main `loop()` function, read the analog signal from the sensor and use the `loop()` function to print the converted result:

```
void loop() {
  reading = analogRead(SENSOR);
  Serial.print("Degrees C:");
  Serial.println(convertToCelsius(reading));
  delay(TEMPERATURE_POLL_PERIOD);
}
```

If we upload the sketch and open the serial monitor, we'll notice the current room temperature. Indeed, if we put our finger around the sensor, we will see an increase in the previously detected temperature immediately. The following screenshot is an example of the sketch output:

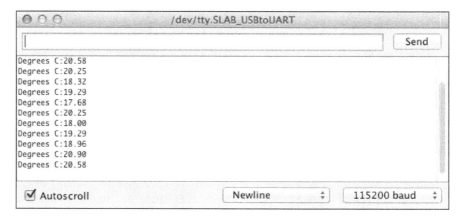

Sending data and receiving commands

The next step is to enable the ADK communication as usual, and we need to add the *accessory descriptor* code at the top of the sketch as follows:

```
#include <adk.h>
#define BUFFSIZE 128
char accessoryName[] = "Chronotherm";
char manufacturer[] = "Example, Inc.";
char model[] = "Chronotherm";
char versionNumber[] = "0.1.0";
char serialNumber[] = "1";
char url[] = "http://www.example.com";
uint8_t buffer[BUFFSIZE];
uint32_t readBytes = 0;
USBHost Usb;
ADK adk(&Usb, manufacturer, model, accessoryName, versionNumber,
url, serialNumber);
```

Now we have to send the detected float temperature back to the Android application, like we did in *Chapter 5, Managing Interactions with Physical Components*. To load the buffer with a float number and send the value through the internal bus, we have to add a `writeToAdk()` helper function with the following code:

```
void writeToAdk(float temperature) {
  char tempBuffer[BUFFSIZE];
  sprintf(tempBuffer, "%f", temperature);
  memcpy(buffer, tempBuffer, BUFFSIZE);
  adk.write(strlen(tempBuffer), buffer);
}
```

The preceding function expects a float temperature converted from the sensor reading. We use the `sprintf()` function call to fill a temporary buffer and then use the `memcpy()` function to replace the ADK buffer content with the `tempBuffer` variable. When the loading is done, we send the buffer contents to the Android application.

During the main `loop()` function, we also need to listen to any commands sent by Android that describe the need to turn on or off the boiler. For this reason, we need to create an executor function like we did in *Chapter 2, Know your Tools*. Then, we have to read commands from the ADK and pass the result to the executor. To achieve this, we need to perform the following steps:

1. Add the `executor()` function that reads a command and turns the external device on or off:

```
void executor(uint8_t command) {
  switch(command) {
    case 0:
      digitalWrite(BOILER, LOW);
      break;
    case 1:
      digitalWrite(BOILER, HIGH);
      break;
    default:
      // noop
      break;
  }
}
```

2. Add the `executeFromAdk()` function that reads a command from the ADK and passes that command to the preceding `executor()` function:

```
void executeFromAdk() {
  adk.read(&readBytes, BUFFSIZE, buffer);
  if (readBytes > 0){
    executor(buffer[0]);
  }
}
```

If we take a look at the plan defined at the beginning of the chapter, we have all the required components for the Arduino sketch, so we can put everything together in the main `loop()` function using the following code:

```
void loop() {
  Usb.Task();
  if (adk.isReady()) {
    reading = analogRead(SENSOR);
    writeToAdk(convertToCelsius(reading));
    executeFromAdk();
    delay(DELAY);
  }
}
```

When the ADK is ready, we read the sensor value and write its Celsius degrees conversion in the ADK buffer. We then expect a command from the ADK and, if it's available, we execute that command turning the boiler on or off. Now that the sketch is completed, we can proceed writing the Chronotherm Android application.

Managing the chronotherm through Android

When we're building physical applications through the UDOO platform, we have to bear in mind that we can make use of Android components and services to enhance the quality of our projects. Moreover, Android UI elements are more user-friendly and maintainable than the hardware counterpart. For this reason, we will create a software component to manage temperature setpoints instead of the use of potentiometers.

To begin the application prototyping, open Android Studio and start a new application named **Chronotherm** with Android API 19. During the bootstrap process, choose a **Blank Activity** called *Overview*.

Setting up the ADK Toolkit

Before we proceed with the application layout, we need to configure the ADKToolkit for internal communication. Remember to follow these reminders to achieve the correct configuration:

1. Add the *ADKToolkit* library dependency in the `app/build.gradle` file.

2. Sync your Gradle configuration.

3. Create the accessory filter file `usb_accessory_filter.xml` under `res/xml/` with the following code:

   ```
   <resources>
     <usb-accessory
       version="0.1.0"
       model="Chronotherm"
       manufacturer="Example, Inc."/>
   </resources>
   ```

4. Add the *USB accessory support* option requirement and the *USB accessory intent filter* option in the `AndroidManifest.xml` file.

5. In the `Overview.java` class file, declare the `AdkManager` object at the top of the class.

6. Add the `AdkManager` object initialization inside the `onCreate()` method of the `Overview` activity class.

7. Override the `onResume()` activity callback to start the ADK connection when the activity is opening. In this project, we don't close the ADK connection in the `onPause()` callback because we will use two different activities and the connection should remain active.

With the ADK communication up and running, we may proceed and write the Chronotherm user interface.

Designing the Android user interface

The next step is designing the Chronotherm application's user interface to handle the proper feedback together with setpoints management. We will achieve these requirements writing two different Android activities with the following responsibilities:

- An *Overview* activity showing the current time, the detected temperature, and the current boiler status. It should include a widget showing the user's setpoints for each hour of the day. These setpoints are used to decide whether to turn the boiler on or off.

- A *Settings* activity used to change the current setpoints for each hour of the day. This activity should use the same widget of the Overview activity to represent the temperature setpoints.

We begin the implementation starting with the Overview activity and the temperature setpoints widget.

Writing the Overview activity

This activity should provide all details regarding the current status of the Chronotherm application. All the required components are summarized in the following mock-up that defines the order in which the components will be created:

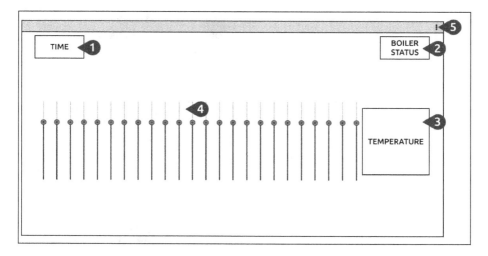

The first step is to update the activity layout, and following the suggestion in the preceding mock-up, we should go through the following steps:

1. At the top of the layout, we could include a `TextClock` view that shows the current system time.

2. The top bar should provide a feedback for the boiler status. We can add a gray `TextView` with the **Active** text that becomes green when the boiler is turned on.

3. The `Overview` body must provide the current detected temperature. Because this is one of the most important details provided by the Chronotherm application, we will emphasize this value making it bigger than other components.

4. Near the room temperature, we will create a widget for the current activated schedule through a set of vertical bars that show the user's setpoints for each hour of the day. In the `Overview` activity, this widget will remain in read-only mode only to provide a quick overview of the active program.

5. In the activity action bar, we should provide a menu item that opens the `Settings` activity. This activity will be used to store setpoints within the Chronotherm application.

We begin the `Overview` implementation starting from the top bar and the detected temperature components; the following steps are required to achieve the preceding layout:

1. In the `res/values/dimens.xml` file, add the following highlighted resources:

```xml
<resources>
    <dimen name="activity_horizontal_margin">16dp</dimen>
    <dimen name="activity_vertical_margin">16dp</dimen>
    <dimen name="text_title">40sp</dimen>
    <dimen name="temperature">100sp</dimen>
    <dimen name="temperature_round">300dp</dimen>
    <dimen name="circle_round">120dp</dimen>
</resources>
```

2. In the `res/values/styles.xml` file, add the following resources and change the `AppTheme` parent attribute as follows:

```xml
<resources>
    <color name="mine_shaft">#444444</color>
    <color name="pistachio">#99CC00</color>
    <color name="coral_red">#FF4444</color>
    <style name="AppTheme" parent="Theme.AppCompat"></style>
</resources>
```

3. To emphasize the current detected temperature, we can create a circle shape that should surround the temperature value. To realize it, create the `circle.xml` file under `res/drawable/` with the following code:

```
<shape
  xmlns:android="http://schemas.android.com/apk/res/
  android"
  android:shape="oval">

  <stroke
    android:width="2dp"
    android:color="@color/coral_red"/>

  <size
    android:width="@dimen/circle_round"
    android:height="@dimen/circle_round"/>
</shape>
```

4. We can now proceed and replace the layout in the `activity_overview.xml` file under `res/layout/`, with the following highlighted code:

```
<LinearLayout
xmlns:android="http://schemas.android.com/apk/res/android"
  xmlns:tools="http://schemas.android.com/tools"
  android:orientation="vertical"
  android:layout_width="match_parent"
  android:layout_height="match_parent"
  android:paddingLeft="@dimen/activity_horizontal_margin"
  android:paddingRight="@dimen/activity_horizontal_margin"
  android:paddingTop="@dimen/activity_vertical_margin"
  android:paddingBottom="@dimen/activity_vertical_margin"
  tools:context=".Overview">
</LinearLayout>
```

5. Place the following code in the preceding `LinearLayout` to create the activity top bar, which contains the current system time and the boiler status:

```
<LinearLayout
  android:layout_width="match_parent"
  android:layout_height="wrap_content">

  <TextClock
    android:textSize="@dimen/text_title"
    android:layout_width="wrap_content"
    android:layout_height="wrap_content" />
```

```
  <TextView
    android:id="@+id/boiler_status"
    android:text="ACTIVE"
    android:gravity="end"
    android:textColor="@color/mine_shaft"
    android:textSize="@dimen/text_title"
    android:layout_width="match_parent"
    android:layout_height="wrap_content" />
</LinearLayout>
```

6. The next step is to create the activity body. It should contain two different items: the first is a `LinearLayout`, where we will inflate the setpoints widget using the `LayoutInflater` class in the activity `onCreate()` callback, and the second is the current detected temperature surrounded by the circle shape we created before. In the root `LinearLayout`, nest the following elements:

```
<LinearLayout
  android:orientation="horizontal"
  android:gravity="center"
  android:layout_width="match_parent"
  android:layout_height="match_parent">

  <LinearLayout
    android:id="@+id/view_container"
    android:gravity="center"
    android:orientation="horizontal"
    android:layout_width="0dp"
    android:layout_weight="1"
    android:layout_height="match_parent">
  </LinearLayout>

  <TextView
    android:id="@+id/temperature"
    android:text="20.5°"
    android:background="@drawable/circle"
    android:gravity="center"
    android:textColor="@color/coral_red"
    android:textSize="@dimen/temperature"
    android:layout_width="@dimen/temperature_round"
    android:layout_height="@dimen/temperature_round" />
</LinearLayout>
```

7. As last steps, store all the view references in the activity code. At the top of the Overview class, add the reference for the temperature and boiler_status views views with the highlighted code:

```
private AdkManager mAdkManager;
private TextView mTemperature;
private TextView mStatus;
```

8. In the Overview onCreate() callback, get the references with the following code:

```
super.onCreate(savedInstanceState);
setContentView(R.layout.activity_overview);
mTemperature = (TextView) findViewById(R.id.temperature);
mStatus = (TextView) findViewById(R.id.boiler_status);
```

These steps provide a partial layout that we will complete adding the setpoints widget and the settings menu item.

Creating a custom UI component

To keep the user interface lean, usable, and intuitive, we can use a set of vertical bars, such as an audio equalizer, so that users can instantly know the room temperature trend they want to obtain. Android ships with a built-in component called SeekBar that we can use to choose a temperature setpoint. Unfortunately, this component draws a horizontal bar and isn't provided with its vertical counterpart; for this reason, we will extend its default behavior.

Android API 11 and later adds the rotate attribute for each component inside the XML. Even if we use a rotation of 270 degrees to obtain a vertical component, we will have some issues to correctly place one bar next to another. In this case, our initial efforts to customize this component will simplify our work later.

Android offers sophisticated and componentized models for building custom UI elements and we can delve into further details at http://developer.android.com/guide/topics/ui/custom-components.html.

The SeekBar component's customization could be organized as follows:

1. As a first step, we should create a TemperatureBar class implementing the vertical sliding behavior. Most of the changes are related to inherit the SeekBar class while switching the component width with its height.

2. The widget needs an XML layout to be programmatically added from our code. For this reason, we will create a layout that includes the TemperatureBar view, the chosen degrees and the hour related to the bar.

3. When any changes occur to the vertical bar component, the degrees number should be updated. In this step, we will create a listener that propagates bar changes to the degrees component providing proper feedback to the users.

4. Our customized component that includes the `TemperatureBar` class, the degrees and hour views, should be programmatically created for each hour of the day. We will create a utility class that is responsible for inflating the component layout 24 times adding the proper listeners.

We begin writing the vertical `SeekBar` class that could be realized with the following steps:

1. Create a new package in your namespace called `widget`.

2. In the newly created package, add the `TemperatureBar` class that extends the `SeekBar` class implementation while defining the default class constructors as follows:

```
public class TemperatureBar extends SeekBar {
  public TemperatureBar(Context context) {
    super(context);
  }
  public TemperatureBar(Context context, AttributeSet attrs) {
    super(context, attrs);
  }
  public TemperatureBar(Context context, AttributeSet
  attrs, int defStyle) {
    super(context, attrs, defStyle);
  }
}
```

3. Continue the `TemperatureBar` class implementation, adding the draw and measure methods at the bottom of the class:

```
@Override
protected void onSizeChanged(int w, int h, int oldw, int
oldh) {
  super.onSizeChanged(h, w, oldh, oldw);
}


@Override
protected synchronized void onMeasure(int width, int
height) {
  super.onMeasure(height, width);
  setMeasuredDimension(getMeasuredHeight(),
  getMeasuredWidth());
}
```

```
@Override
protected void onDraw(Canvas c) {
  c.rotate(-90);
  c.translate(-getHeight(), 0);
  onSizeChanged(getWidth(), getHeight(), 0, 0);
  super.onDraw(c);
}
```

In the first methods, we're switching the widget width with its height so that we can use this parameter to provide an accurate measurement of the component contents. Then we override the `onDraw()` method called by the Android system during component drawing, by applying a translation to the `SeekBar` canvas and placing it vertically. As the last step, we call the `onSizeChanged` callback once again to resize the component after the canvas translation.

4. Because we have switched the bar width and height, we need to override the `onTouchEvent()` method to use the component height during value calculation. At the bottom of the `TemperatureBar()` class, add the following callback:

```
@Override
public boolean onTouchEvent(MotionEvent event) {
  if (!isEnabled()) {
    return false;
  }
  switch (event.getAction()) {
    case MotionEvent.ACTION_DOWN:
    case MotionEvent.ACTION_MOVE:
    case MotionEvent.ACTION_UP:
      setProgress(getMax() - (int) (getMax() * event.getY()
      / getHeight()));
      onSizeChanged(getWidth(), getHeight(), 0, 0);
      break;
    case MotionEvent.ACTION_CANCEL:
      break;
  }
  return true;
}
```

With the preceding code, we update the component progress every time an `ACTION_DOWN`, `ACTION_MOVE`, or `ACTION_UP` method event occurs. We don't need any other behaviors for the purpose of this project, so we leave the remaining implementation as it is.

Now we can proceed writing the XML layout that hosts the preceding component with a degrees and hour `TextView`. Through the following steps, we can achieve a layout that we will inflate from our utility class:

1. Add the `bar_height` declaration to the `dimens.xml` file under `res/values/`, so we can easily change it in the future if needed:

    ```xml
    <dimen name="activity_horizontal_margin">16dp</dimen>
    <dimen name="activity_vertical_margin">16dp</dimen>
    <dimen name="bar_height">400dp</dimen>
    <dimen name="text_title">40sp</dimen>
    ```

2. Create the `temperature_bar.xml` file under `res/layout/` that contains the widget layout. In this file, we should add this `LinearLayout` as the root element:

    ```xml
    <LinearLayout
    xmlns:android="http://schemas.android.com/apk/res/android"
      android:orientation="vertical"
      android:layout_width="0dp"
      android:layout_weight="1"
      android:layout_height="wrap_content">
    </LinearLayout>
    ```

3. To the preceding `LinearLayout`, include the following components:

    ```xml
    <TextView
      android:id="@+id/degrees"
      android:text="0"
      android:gravity="center"
      android:layout_width="match_parent"
      android:layout_height="match_parent" />

    <me.palazzetti.widget.TemperatureBar
      android:id="@+id/seekbar"
      android:max="40"
      android:layout_gravity="center"
      android:layout_width="wrap_content"
      android:layout_height="@dimen/bar_height" />

    <TextView
      android:id="@+id/time"
      android:text="00"
    ```

```
android:gravity="center"
android:layout_width="match_parent"
android:layout_height="match_parent" />
```

> Always change the me.palazzetti namespace occurrences with your own.

Now that we have the temperature bar component and the widget layout, we need to create a binding between the degrees and the seekbar views. Proceed with the widget implementation through the following steps:

1. Create the DegreeListener class in the widget package.

2. The preceding class should implement the SeekBar listener while storing the reference for the connected degrees view. We use this TextView reference to propagate the vertical bar value:

```
public class DegreeListener implements
SeekBar.OnSeekBarChangeListener {
  private TextView mDegrees;
  public DegreeListener(TextView degrees) {
    mDegrees = degrees;
  }
```

3. Propagate the progress value to the mDegrees view, overriding the following methods required by the OnSeekBarChangeListener interface:

```
@Override
public void onProgressChanged(SeekBar seekBar, int
progress, boolean b) {
  mDegrees.setText(String.valueOf(progress));
}

@Override
public void onStartTrackingTouch(SeekBar seekBar) {}

@Override
public void onStopTrackingTouch(SeekBar seekBar) {}
}
```

The last missing part is to provide the utility class used to inflate the widget layout initializing the TemperatureBar class with the DegreeListener class. The inflate process should be repeated for each hour of the day and it needs the reference of the layout in which the widget will be inflated. To complete the implementation, go through the following steps:

1. Create the TemperatureWidget class in the widget package.

2. This class should expose a static addTo() method that expects the activity context, the parent element, and whether vertical bars should be created in read-only mode. In this way, we can use this widget both for visualization and edit. We can find the complete implementation in the following code snippet:

```
public class TemperatureWidget {
    private static final int BAR_NUMBER = 24;
    public static TemperatureBar[] addTo(Context ctx,
    ViewGroup parent, boolean enabled) {
        TemperatureBar[] bars = new TemperatureBar[BAR_NUMBER];
        for (int i = 0; i < BAR_NUMBER; i++) {
            View v = LayoutInflater.from(ctx).
            inflate(R.layout.temperature_bar, parent, false);
            TextView time = (TextView) v.findViewById(R.id.time);
            TextView degree = (TextView)
            v.findViewById(R.id.degrees);
            TemperatureBar bar = (TemperatureBar)
            v.findViewById(R.id.seekbar);
            time.setText(String.format("%02d", i));
            degree.setText(String.valueOf(0));
            bar.setOnSeekBarChangeListener
            (new DegreeListener(degree));
            bar.setProgress(0);
            bar.setEnabled(enabled);
            parent.addView(v, parent.getChildCount());
            bars[i] = bar;
        }
        return bars;
    }
}
```

At the top of the class, we're defining the generated bar's number. In the addTo() method, we inflate the temperature_bar layout to create an instance of the bar object. Then, we get all the references of time, degrees, and seekbar objects so that we can set initial values and create the DegreeListener class with the degrees TextView binding. We proceed adding the widget to the parent node, filling the bars array with the currently created bar. As the last step, we return this array so that it can be used from the caller activity.

Finishing the Overview activity

The setpoints widget is now completed and we can proceed with the last steps inflating temperature bars during the activity creation. We will also add the action to start the Settings activity in the activity menu. To complete the Overview class, follow these steps:

1. Inflate the setpoints widget in the Overview onCreate() callback by adding the highlighted code:

```
super.onCreate(savedInstanceState);
setContentView(R.layout.activity_overview);
mTemperature = (TextView) findViewById(R.id.temperature);
mStatus = (TextView) findViewById(R.id.boiler_status);
ViewGroup container = (ViewGroup)
findViewById(R.id.view_container);
mBars = TemperatureWidget.addTo(this, container, false);
```

2. Handle the action bar menu to start the Settings activity, changing the onOptionsItemSelected() method as follows:

```
@Override
public boolean onOptionsItemSelected(MenuItem item) {
    int id = item.getItemId();
    if (id == R.id.action_settings) {
        Intent intent = new Intent(this, Settings.class);
        startActivity(intent);
        return true;
    }
    return super.onOptionsItemSelected(item);
}
```

 The Settings activity is not available at the moment and we will create it in the next section.

We've completed the `Overview` class layout and the following screenshot is the obtained result:

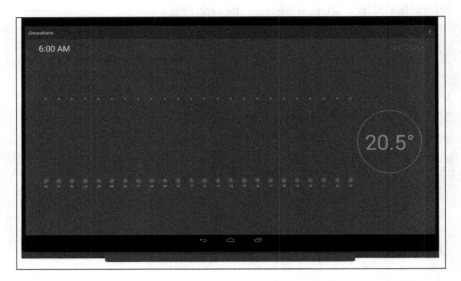

Writing the Settings activity

The next step before implementing the logic of our chronotherm, is to create the `Settings` activity that can be used to change the temperature setpoints during the day. To bootstrap a new activity, click on **File** from the window menu and choose **New** to open the context menu. There, choose **Activity** and then **Blank Activity**. This will open a new window and we can write `Settings` in the **Activity Name** and then click on **Finish**.

Even if we can use the built-in settings template with synchronized preferences, we're using a blank activity to keep this part as easy as possible.

We start designing the activity layout with the following mock-up, showing all the required components:

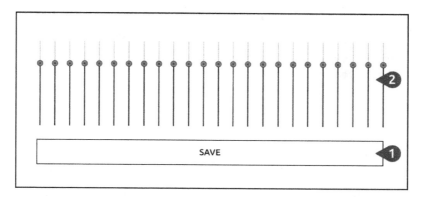

The first required step is to update the activity layout and, following the suggestion in the previous mock-up, we should:

1. Add a **Save** button that will call an activity method to save the selected setpoints from the temperature widgets.

2. Inflate the temperature widget used during the setpoints selection.

To achieve the preceding layout, update the `activity_settings.xml` file under `res/layout/` with the following changes:

1. Replace the root layout element with the following `LinearLayout`:

```
<LinearLayout
xmlns:android="http://schemas.android.com/apk/res/android"
    xmlns:tools="http://schemas.android.com/tools"
    android:orientation="vertical"
    android:layout_width="match_parent"
    android:layout_height="match_parent"
    android:paddingLeft="@dimen/activity_horizontal_margin"
    android:paddingRight="@dimen/activity_horizontal_margin"
    android:paddingTop="@dimen/activity_vertical_margin"
    android:paddingBottom="@dimen/activity_vertical_margin"
    tools:context="me.palazzetti.chronotherm.Settings">
</LinearLayout>
```

2. In the preceding layout, add the widget placeholder and the **Save** button:

```
<LinearLayout
    android:id="@+id/edit_container"
    android:orientation="horizontal"
    android:layout_width="match_parent"
    android:layout_height="wrap_content">
</LinearLayout>

<Button
    android:text="Save settings"
    android:layout_marginTop="50dp"
    android:layout_width="match_parent"
    android:layout_height="wrap_content" />
```

We can complete the activity adding the widget initialization in the Settings class through the following steps:

1. Add the highlighted variable at the top of Settings class:

```
public class Settings extends ActionBarActivity {
    private TemperatureBar[] mBars;
    // ...
```

2. In the onCreate() method of the Settings class, add the highlighted code to inflate the setpoints widget:

```
@Override
protected void onCreate(Bundle savedInstanceState) {
    super.onCreate(savedInstanceState);
    setContentView(R.layout.activity_settings);
    ViewGroup container = (ViewGroup)
    findViewById(R.id.edit_container);
    mBars = TemperatureWidget.addTo(this, container, true);
}
```

If we upload the Android application again, we can use the menu options to open the Settings activity, which presents itself as shown in the following screenshot:

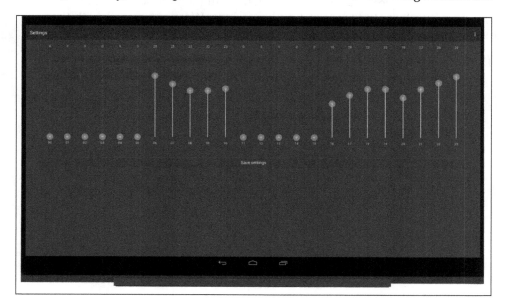

The Chronotherm application's interface is completed and we can proceed managing the storage layer for the user's settings.

Managing user's setpoints

The Chronotherm application's activities provide the required user interface components to show and change the user's setpoints. To let them work, we should implement the logic to save persistent application data. Based on our needs, we can use the SharedPreferences class to store primitive data in key-value pairs to provide setpoint values for the entire application. In this project, we will use the setpoint hour as the key and the chosen temperature as the value.

> SharedPreferences class is a storage option provided by the Android framework. If in other projects we need a different storage, we may take a look at Android's official documentation at developer.android.com/ guide/topics/data/data-storage.html.

Reading setpoints from the Overview activity

We begin with the Overview activity implementing a method that reads stored setpoints and updates the temperature bar values. We can proceed with the following steps reading the user's preferences during the activity creation:

1. For each bar, we set the progress with the stored value. We use 0 as the default when no settings are found. This implementation requires the following code that we should add in the Overview class:

```
private void readPreferences() {
  SharedPreferences sharedPref =
  getSharedPreferences("__CHRONOTHERM__",
  Context.MODE_PRIVATE);
  for (int i = 0; i < mBars.length; i++) {
    int value = sharedPref.getInt(String.valueOf(i), 0);
    mBars[i].setProgress(value);
  }
}
```

We open the application's preferences and update each bar using the hour of the day as a key. The related hour is indirectly represented by the i loop counter.

2. Call the preceding method from the onResume() activity callback, adding the highlighted code:

```
protected void onResume() {
  super.onResume();
  readPreferences();
  mAdkManager.open();
}
```

Through these steps, we've completed setpoints management in the Overview activity and we will proceed working with the Settings activity.

Writing setpoints from the Settings activity

In the Settings activity, we should implement the logic to store the users setpoints when they click on the **Save settings** button. Moreover, when the activity is created, we must load the previously stored setpoints so that we can present the current schedule to the users before they start changing their preferences. To implement these functionalities, we may proceed with the following steps:

1. Like we did in the `Overview` activity, we need to load setpoint values and update temperature bars. Because we've already implemented this functionality, we can simply copy and paste the `readPreferences()` method as is from the `Overview` class to the `Settings` class.

2. Add the following code at the bottom of the `Settings` class to store the selected setpoints:

```
public void savePreferences(View v) {
    SharedPreferences sharedPref =
    getSharedPreferences("chronotherm",
    Context.MODE_PRIVATE);
    SharedPreferences.Editor editor = sharedPref.edit();
    for (int i = 0; i < mBars.length; i ++) {
        editor.putInt(String.valueOf(i),
        mBars[i].getProgress());
    }
    editor.apply();
    this.finish();
}
```

   After we've retrieved and stored all setpoints using a background commit, we close the current activity.

3. In the `activity_settings.xml` layout file under `res/layout/`, update the save button so that it will call the preceding method on click, as you can see in the following highlighted code:

```
<Button
    android:onClick="savePreferences"
    android:text="Save settings"
    android:layout_marginTop="50dp"
    android:layout_width="match_parent"
    android:layout_height="wrap_content" />
```

This was the last step to implement the Chronotherm application interface and settings management. Now we can proceed implementing the required logic to read the detected temperature and to turn the boiler on or off.

Interacting with Arduino

Our application is ready to receive temperature data checking whether the boiler should be activated or not. The overall design is to use the `ExecutorService` class that runs a periodical scheduled thread and it should:

1. Read the detected temperature from ADK.

2. Update the boiler status checking whether the temperature is below the current selected setpoint.

3. Send the temperature to the main thread so that it can update the temperature `TextView`.

4. Send the command to Arduino to turn the boiler on or off. This task should be done only if the current boiler status has changed from the previous task execution. In this case, it should also send the boiler status to the main thread so that it can update the related `TextView`.

Before we proceed with thread implementation, we should provide a Java interface that exposes the required methods to update the activity's user interface. We can fulfill this with the following steps:

1. Create a new Java interface called `OnDataChangeListener` and add the following code snippet:

    ```
    public interface OnDataChangeListener {
      void onTemperatureChanged(float temperature);
      void onBoilerChanged(boolean status);
    }
    ```

2. Add the preceding interface to the `Overview` class using the highlighted code:

    ```
    public class Overview extends ActionBarActivity implements
    OnDataChangeListener {
    ```

3. Implement the interface by writing the code that updates the current temperature and the boiler status TextViews:

    ```
    @Override
    public void onTemperatureChanged(float temperature) {
      mTemperature.setText(String.format("%.1f°",
      temperature));
    }

    @Override
    public void onBoilerChanged(boolean status) {
      if (status) {
    ```

```
      mStatus.setTextColor(getResources().getColor
      (R.color.pistachio));
    }
    else {
      mStatus.setTextColor(getResources().getColor
      (R.color.mine_shaft));
    }
  }
```

Now we can proceed implementing the scheduled thread, following the overall design explained previously:

1. Create a new package in your namespace called `adk`.

2. In the `adk` package, add a new class named `DataReader`.

3. At the top of the class, add the following declarations:
   ```
   private final static int TEMPERATURE_POLLING = 1000;
   private final static int TEMPERATURE_UPDATED = 0;
   private final static int BOILER_UPDATED = 1;
   private AdkManager mAdkManager;
   private Context mContext;
   private OnDataChangeListener mCaller;
   private ScheduledExecutorService mSchedulerSensor;
   private Handler mMainLoop;
   boolean mBoilerStatus = false;
   ```

   We define the polling time for the scheduled thread and the message types used in the main thread handler to identify a temperature or a boiler update. We store the references for the `AdkManager` instance, the activity context, and the caller activity that implements the previous interface. Then we define the `ExecutorService` implementation that we will use to create short-lived threads for sensor readings.

4. Implement the `DataReader` constructor to set the message handler when the main thread receives messages from the sensor thread:
   ```
   public DataReader(AdkManager adkManager, Context ctx,
   OnDataChangeListener caller) {
     this.mAdkManager = adkManager;
     this.mContext = ctx;
     this.mCaller = caller;
     mMainLoop = new Handler(Looper.getMainLooper()) {
       @Override
       public void handleMessage(Message message) {
         switch (message.what) {
           case TEMPERATURE_UPDATED:
   ```

```
      mCaller.onTemperatureChanged((float)
      message.obj);
      break;
    case BOILER_UPDATED:
      mCaller.onBoilerChanged((boolean) message.obj);
      break;
    }
  }
};
}
```

We store all the required references and then we define the main thread handler. Within the handler, we use the OnDataChangeListener callbacks to update the temperature or the boiler status in the view, according to the message type.

5. At the bottom of the DataReader constructor, add the following Runnable method implementation that realizes the overall design previously defined:

```
private class SensorThread implements Runnable {
  @Override
  public void run() {
    Message message;
    // Reads from ADK and check boiler status
    AdkMessage response = mAdkManager.read();
    float temperature = response.getFloat();
    boolean status = isBelowSetpoint(temperature);
    // Updates temperature back to the main thread
    message = mMainLoop.obtainMessage(TEMPERATURE_UPDATED,
    temperature);
    message.sendToTarget();
    // Turns on/off the boiler and updates the status
    if (mBoilerStatus != status) {
      int adkCommand = status ? 1 : 0;
      mAdkManager.write(adkCommand);
      message = mMainLoop.obtainMessage(BOILER_UPDATED,
      status);
      message.sendToTarget();
      mBoilerStatus = status;
    }
  }
  private boolean isBelowSetpoint(float temperature) {
    SharedPreferences sharedPref =
    mContext.getSharedPreferences("__CHRONOTHERM__",
    Context.MODE_PRIVATE);
```

```
    int currentHour =
    Calendar.getInstance().get(Calendar.HOUR_OF_DAY);
    return temperature <
    sharedPref.getInt(String.valueOf(currentHour), 0);
  }
}
```

In this implementation, we create the `isBelowSetpoint()` method that checks whether the temperature is below the chosen setpoint for the current hour. We retrieve this value from the application's shared preferences.

6. Add a method to the `DataReader` class to start the scheduler that spawns short-lived threads periodically as follows:

```
public void start() {
  // Start thread that listens to ADK
  SensorThread sensor = new SensorThread();
  mSchedulerSensor =
  Executors.newSingleThreadScheduledExecutor();
  mSchedulerSensor.scheduleAtFixedRate(sensor, 0,
  TEMPERATURE_POLLING, TimeUnit.MILLISECONDS);
}
```

7. Add the `stop()` method at the bottom of the class to stop the scheduler from spawning new threads through the `shutdown()` executor's method:

```
public void stop() {
  mSchedulerSensor.shutdown();
}
```

8. Now we should go back to the `Overview` class to start and stop the scheduler within the activity lifecycle. Add the `DataReader` declaration at the top of the `Overview` class:

```
private AdkManager mAdkManager;
private DataReader mReader;
```

9. Initialize the `DataReader` instance in the `onCreate()` callback through the following highlighted code:

```
    mAdkManager = new AdkManager(this);
    mReader = new DataReader(mAdkManager, this, this);
}
```

10. Start and stop the reading scheduler in the `onResume()` and `onPause()` activity's callbacks, as you can see in the highlighted code:

```
@Override
protected void onPause() {
  super.onPause();
  mReader.stop();
}

@Override
protected void onResume() {
  super.onResume();
  readPreferences();
  mAdkManager.open();
  mReader.start();
}
```

The communication between UDOO and Android is up and running and the logic of our chronotherm is ready to activate and deactivate the boiler. Now, we can upload the Android application again, add some temperature settings, and start playing with the prototype. We've completed our prototype and the last missing task is to update the application version in the `app/build.gradle` file with a `0.1.0` version, as you can see in the following code:

```
defaultConfig {
  applicationId "me.palazzetti.chronotherm"
  minSdkVersion 19
  targetSdkVersion 21
  versionCode 1
  versionName "0.1.0"
}
```

Improving the prototype

During this chapter we've made different design decisions making the chronotherm easier to implement. While this application is good proof of concept for home automation, we have to bear in mind that many things should be done to improve the quality and reliability of the prototype. This application is a classical scenario with a **Human-Machine Interface (HMI)** and a **Control System** implemented respectively, with an Android application and an Arduino microcontroller. In such scenarios, a driving principle of automation design is that the control unit should be capable of making *reasonable and safe decisions* even in the absence of the HMI part.

In our case, we've decoupled responsibilities delegating the decision to turn the boiler on or off to the Android application. While this isn't a mission-critical system, with this design, we may risk that if the Android application crashes, the boiler remains turned on forever. A better decoupling would be using the HMI only for showing feedback and storing the user's setpoints, while the decision to change the boiler status remains in the control unit. This means that instead of sending on or off commands to Arduino, we should send the current setpoint that will be stored in the microcontroller's memory. In this way, the control unit could make safe choices according to the last received setpoint.

Another improvement that we may take into account as an exercise is to implement a **hysteresis logic**. Our chronotherm is designed to turn the boiler on or off, respectively, when the detected temperature exceeds or is below the chosen setpoint. This behavior should be improved because with such design, when the temperature is stabilized around the setpoint, the chronotherm will start to turn the boiler on and off very frequently. We can find useful details and suggestions about applying hysteresis logic in control systems at http://en.wikipedia.org/wiki/Hysteresis#Control_systems.

Summary

In this chapter, we explored the land of home automation and how UDOO can be used to work out some daily tasks. You learned about the advantages of using smart objects that are capable of solving place and time problems when you aren't at home. Then, we planned a chronotherm prototype to control our living room temperature through a sensor. To make the device fully automated, we designed a use case where users can decide temperature setpoints for each hour of the day.

At the beginning, we built the application circuit using a temperature sensor and an LED to simulate the boiler. We started programming the Android user interface customizing a regular UI component to fit our needs better. We started writing the overview activity that showed the current time, the boiler status, the current room temperature, and the widget with chosen setpoints for the whole day. We continued with the settings activity used to store the chronotherm temperature schedule. As the last step, we wrote a scheduled thread that reads the environment temperature and turns the boiler on or off, matching the detected temperature with the current setpoint.

In the next chapter, we will extend this prototype with new functionalities to enhance the human interaction thanks to a powerful set of Android APIs.

7
Using Android APIs for Human Interaction

The advent of personal computers in the 1980s started a new challenge: making computers and computation useful for and usable by hobbyists, students, and, in more general terms, technology enthusiasts. These people needed an easy way to control their machines, so human and computer interaction quickly became an open research field aimed at improving usability and resulting in the development of graphical user interfaces and new input devices. In the last decade, other interaction patterns such as voice recognition, voice synthesis, motion tracking, and many others were used in commercial applications, a great improvement that indirectly caused the evolution of objects such as phones, tablets, and glasses into a new kind of smarter devices.

The goal of this chapter is to take advantage of these new interaction patterns using a subset of Android APIs enhancing the Chronotherm prototype with a new set of features, thus making it a little bit smarter.

In this chapter, we will cover the following topics:

- Extending prototypes with Android APIs
- Using voice recognition to control our prototype
- Giving feedback to users through voice synthesis

Extending prototypes with Android APIs

The Chronotherm application is designed to turn on a boiler when the detected temperature exceeds the user's temperature setpoint. In the previous prototype, we created a settings page in which users can set their preferences for each hour of the day. We can extend the prototype behavior, giving our users the ability to store more than one setpoint configuration. In this way, we could provide preset management that users can activate according to different factors such as the day of the week or the current season.

While adding this feature, we have to bear in mind that this isn't a desktop application, so we should avoid the creation of a new bunch of overwhelming user interfaces. The Chronotherm application could be deployed in the users home and, because they are usually noiseless places, we can take into consideration the use of **voice recognition** to get the users input. This approach will remove the need for other activities to create or edit stored presets. In the meantime, we have to take into account that we need to provide feedback when the voice recognition process ends so that users know whether their command was accepted or not. Even if we can solve this problem using small popups or notifications, we can provide a better user experience using **voice synthesis** to give feedback to our users.

> Voice recognition and synthesis are features that we can use to give a new kind of interaction to our applications. However, we have to bear in mind that these components could create serious accessibility issues for people with visual, physical, or hearing loss limitations. Every time we want to create a good project, we have to work really hard to make beautiful applications that can be used by everyone. Android helps us a lot with the **accessibility framework**, so, for future projects, remember to follow all best practices available at https://developer.android.com/guide/topics/ui/accessibility/index.html.

The Android SDK exposes a set of APIs that we can use to interact with the installed text-to-speech service and voice input methods, but **Vanilla Android** shipped in UDOO does not provide them out of the box. For our code to work, we need to install an application for voice recognition and another one implementing text-to-speech functionalities.

For example, almost any Android device on the market comes with such applications already installed as part of the **Google Mobile Services** suite. For more details on this topic, follow the link http://www.udoo.org/guide-how-to-install-gapps-on-udoo-running-android/.

Improving user settings

Before we proceed with our implementation of the voice recognition service, we need to change how settings are stored in our physical application. At the moment, we're using the Chronotherm application's shared preferences in which we store the chosen setpoint for each SeekBar class. According to new requirements, this is no longer suitable for our application because we need to persist different setpoints for each preset. Moreover, we need to persist the current activated preset and all these changes force us to design a new user interface together with a new settings system.

We can take a look at the following screenshot to find what changes we should take:

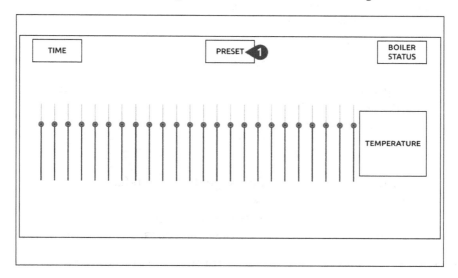

The first required step is to update our user interface. Following the suggestion in the above mock-up, we should:

1. Add a new TextView at the top of the layout that shows the name of the current preset. The name should be changed while loading the activity and whenever the user activates a new preset.

To achieve the preceding layout, update the activity_overview.xml file under res/layout/ with the following changes inside the header LinearLayout where the TextClock and the boiler_status views are located:

1. Change the TextClock view, replacing the layout_width attribute with the highlighted code and adding the layout_weight attribute:

    ```
    android:layout_width="0dp"
    android:layout_weight="1"
    ```

2. Change the layout of the `boiler_status` TextView as we did in the previous step:

```
android:layout_width="0dp"
android:layout_weight="1"
```

3. Add the following TextView between the preceding components to show the activated preset:

```
<TextView
  android:id="@+id/current_preset"
  android:text="NO PRESET ACTIVATED"
  android:gravity="center"
  android:textColor="@color/coral_red"
  android:textSize="@dimen/text_title"
  android:layout_width="0dp"
  android:layout_weight="2"
  android:layout_height="match_parent" />
```

4. At the top of the `Overview` class, add the reference for the `current_preset` view with the highlighted code:

```
private TextView mCurrentPreset;
private TextView mTemperature;
private TextView mStatus;
```

5. In the `Overview` `onCreate` callback, get the view reference with the following code:

```
setContentView(R.layout.activity_overview);
mCurrentPreset = (TextView) findViewById(R.id.current_preset);
```

The following screenshot is what we obtain through the preceding layout:

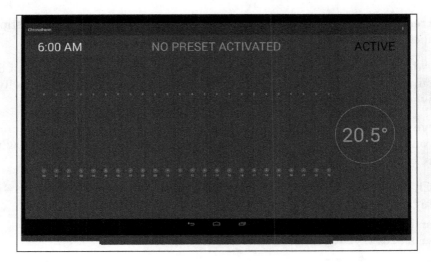

Storing preset configurations

As previously discussed, we should change how user setpoints are stored and retrieved within the Chronotherm application. The idea is to isolate access to the application's shared preferences in a new `Preset` class that exposes the following methods:

- A `set()` method to save a setpoint configuration corresponding to a preset name. The array of setpoint values is serialized in a comma-separated string and saved using the preset name as the key.

- A `get()` method to return stored setpoints for the given preset name. The setpoint string is deserialized and returned as an array of values.

- A `getCurrent()` method to return the name of the latest activated preset.

- A `setCurrent()` method to promote the given preset name as the latest activated preset.

To create the `Preset` class, proceed with the following steps:

1. Create the `Preset` class in the `chronotherm` package.

2. Add the following declarations at the top of the `Preset` class:

```
private static final String SHARED_PREF =
"__CHRONOTHERM__";
private static final String CURRENT_PRESET = "__CURRENT__";
private static final String NO_PRESET = "NO PRESET
ACTIVATED";
```

We put the preferences name we used in the previous chapter in a variable called `SHARED_PREF`. The `CURRENT_PRESET` key is used to get or set the currently used preset. The `NO_PRESET` assignment defines the value that is returned by default when no presets are found. This handles the first application run case showing the **NO PRESET ACTIVATED** screen when no preset is found.

3. Add the `set()` method at the bottom of the `Preset` class:

```
public static void set(Context ctx, String name,
ArrayList<Integer> values) {
    SharedPreferences sharedPref =
    ctx.getSharedPreferences(SHARED_PREF,
    Context.MODE_PRIVATE);
    SharedPreferences.Editor editor = sharedPref.edit();
    String serializedValues = TextUtils.join(",", values);
    editor.putString(name, serializedValues);
    editor.apply();
}
```

The preceding method expects the `values` array that represents the user's setpoints for the given preset `name` variable. We use the `TextUtils` class to serialize the values array in a comma-separated string while using the preset `name` variable as the key.

4. Add the `get()` method at the bottom of the `Preset` class:

```
public static ArrayList<Integer> get(Context ctx, String
name) {
   ArrayList<Integer> values = new ArrayList<Integer>();
   SharedPreferences sharedPref =
   ctx.getSharedPreferences(SHARED_PREF,
   Context.MODE_PRIVATE);   String serializedValues = sharedPref.
getString(name,
   null);
   if (serializedValues != null) {
     for (String progress : serializedValues.split(",")) {
       values.add(Integer.valueOf(progress));
     }
   }
   return values;
}
```

We fill the `values` array with the setpoints retrieved through the preset `name` variable. We know the values are comma-serialized, so we split and parse the string, adding each value to the preceding array. If we do not find any match with the given preset `name` variable, we return an empty array.

5. Add the `getCurrent()` method at the bottom of the class to return the currently activated preset:

```
public static String getCurrent(Context ctx) {
   String currentPreset;
   SharedPreferences sharedPref =
   ctx.getSharedPreferences(SHARED_PREF,
   Context.MODE_PRIVATE);
   currentPreset = sharedPref.getString(CURRENT_PRESET,
   NO_PRESET);
   return currentPreset;
}
```

6. Add the `setCurrent()` method at the bottom of the class to store the currently activated preset:

```
public static void setCurrent(Context ctx, String name) {
   SharedPreferences sharedPref =
   ctx.getSharedPreferences(SHARED_PREF,
   Context.MODE_PRIVATE);
```

```
SharedPreferences.Editor editor = sharedPref.edit();
editor.putString(CURRENT_PRESET, name);
editor.apply();
}
```

Now that we have a formal representation of the user's presets, we should adapt both the activities to reflect the latest changes.

Using presets among activities

We begin with the Overview activity that should load the current preset during the activity's resuming phase. If a preset is activated, we should change the current_preset TextView with the preset name. To achieve this step, we should replace the readPreferences method with the following code:

```
private void readPreferences() {
    String activatedPreset = Preset.getCurrent(this);
    mCurrentValues = Preset.get(this, activatedPreset);
    for (int i = 0; i < mCurrentValues.size(); i++) {
        mBars[i].setProgress(mCurrentValues.get(i));
    }
    mCurrentPreset.setText(activatedPreset.toUpperCase());
}
```

The next step is to adapt the Settings activity with a new behavior, summarized in the following steps:

1. When users open the Settings activity, the voice recognition system should ask for preset name.

2. If the given preset is found, we should load the preset's setpoints and update all temperature bars. When users save the new preferences, the old setpoints are updated.

3. If the given preset is not found, there is no need to update the temperature bars. When users save the new preferences, a new preset entry is stored with the given setpoints.

We still don't have all the components needed to implement the first step because we're missing the voice recognition implementation. In the meantime, we can update how presets are stored and retrieved in this activity through the following steps:

1. At the top of the class, add the highlighted variable that will store the recognized preset name:

```
private TemperatureBar[] mBars;
private String mEditingPreset;
```

2. In the `onCreate()` callback of the `Settings` activity, remove the `readPreferences()` method's call.

3. Update the `readPreferences()` member function so it loads values for the given preset name (when available) and returns values denoting whether this preset is found or not. We can implement this behavior with the following code:

```
private boolean readPreferences(String presetName) {
  boolean found;
  ArrayList<Integer> values;
  values = Preset.get(this, presetName);
  found = values.size() > 0;
  for (int i = 0; i < values.size(); i ++) {
    mBars[i].setProgress(values.get(i));
  }
  return found;
}
```

4. Update the `savePreferences()` method so it uses the `Preset` class to store or update the given setpoints:

```
public void savePreferences(View v) {
  ArrayList<Integer> values = new ArrayList<Integer>();
  for (int i = 0; i < mBars.length; i++) {
    values.add(mBars[i].getProgress());
  }
  Preset.set(this, mEditingPreset, values);
  this.finish();
}
```

Through these steps, we have changed preset management in both activities. We still need to complete the `Settings` activity because we're missing the recognition phase. We will complete these steps later, after the implementation of voice recognition.

The last, missing step in adapting the Chronotherm application to the new preset management is to change the temperature check in the `SensorThread` parameter. Indeed, the `isBelowSetpoint` method should retrieve the values of the activated preset matching this setpoint with the last temperature reading. If any preset is selected, it should turn off the boiler by default. We could achieve this behavior by changing the `isBelowSetpoint` method with the highlighted code:

```
private boolean isBelowSetpoint(float temperature) {
  int currentHour =
  Calendar.getInstance().get(Calendar.HOUR_OF_DAY);
  String currentPreset = Preset.getCurrent(mContext);
  ArrayList<Integer> currentValues = Preset.get(mContext,
  currentPreset);
  if (currentValues.size() > 0) {
    return temperature < currentValues.get(currentHour);
  }
  else {
    return false;
  }
}
```

This ends the `Preset` configuration process and now we can proceed with implementing voice recognition.

Implementing voice recognition

Now that our prototype can handle different presets, we should provide a fast way to change, create, or edit user presets through voice recognition. One of the easiest ways to manage voice recognition is to use Android's `Intent` messaging object to delegate this action to another application component. As we discussed at the beginning of the chapter, if we install and configure a compliant voice input application, Android can use it for voice recognition.

The main goal is to provide an abstract class that will be extended by our activities in order to manage recognition callback, while avoiding code repetition. The overall design is as follows:

- We should provide a common interface for activities that need voice recognition.
- We should provide a `startRecognition()` method to launch the recognition activity through the `Intent` object.

- We should implement the `onActivityResult()` callback that will be called by the launched activity when voice recognition ends. In this callback, we use the best among all the results produced during the voice recognition process.

 Job delegation is one of the most useful features of the Android operating system. If you need more information about how it works under the hood, take a look at the Android official documentation at http://developer.android.com/guide/components/intents-filters.html.

The preceding abstraction to reuse voice recognition capability can be achieved with the following steps:

1. Add in the `IRecognitionListener` interface in the `chronotherm` package that defines the `onRecognitionDone()` callback used to send back the result to the caller activity. We can achieve this with the following code:

```
public interface IRecognitionListener {
  void onRecognitionDone(int requestCode, String
  bestMatch);
}
```

2. Create a new package called `voice` and add a new abstract class called `RecognizerActivity`. This class should be defined as follows:

```
public abstract class RecognizerActivity extends
ActionBarActivity implements IRecognitionListener {
}
```

3. Add a public method to initialize the recognition phase, delegating the responsibility for retrieving the results, with the following code:

```
public void startRecognition(String what, int requestCode)
{
  Intent intent = new
  Intent(RecognizerIntent.ACTION_RECOGNIZE_SPEECH);
  intent.putExtra(RecognizerIntent.EXTRA_LANGUAGE,
  "en-US");
  intent.putExtra(RecognizerIntent.EXTRA_PROMPT, what);
  startActivityForResult(intent, requestCode);
}
```

The `requestCode` parameter is the recognition `Intent` identifier and is used by the caller activity to properly identify the result and how to handle it. The `what` parameter is used to provide an on-screen message if the external application supports it.

4. Add the `onActivityResult()` callback to extract the best result and pass it to the caller activity through the common interface:

```
@Override
protected void onActivityResult(int requestCode, int resultCode,
Intent data) {
  if (resultCode == RESULT_OK) {
    ArrayList<String> matches =
    data.getStringArrayListExtra
    (RecognizerIntent.EXTRA_RESULTS);
      this.onRecognitionDone(requestCode, matches.get(0));
  }
}
```

Using voice recognition to add or edit presets

Through the `RecognizerActivity` class, we delegate the hard work to the Android framework. According to the nature of the activity, we should handle results in different ways. We start using voice inputs with the `Settings` activity asking the name of the preset we want to create or edit during the activity creation phase. If the preset exists, we should load stored setpoints and update them during the save process. Otherwise, we should create a new record in our preferences. To achieve this behavior, perform the following steps:

1. From the `Settings` class, extend `RecognizerActivity` in line with the following snippet:

```
public class Settings extends RecognizerActivity {
  //...
}
```

2. Declare the intent request code that we will use to identify and handle the recognized result. At the top of the class, add the highlighted code:

```
public class Settings extends RecognizerActivity {
  private static final int VOICE_SETTINGS = 1001;
  private TemperatureBar[] mBars;
  // ...
}
```

3. At the bottom of the `onCreate()` callback, add the following code to start voice recognition as soon as possible:

```
mBars = TemperatureWidget.addTo(this, container, true);
startRecognition("Choose the preset you want to edit",
VOICE_SETTINGS);
```

4. Implement the `onRecognitionDone()` callback, required by the
   `IRecognitionListener` interface previously defined, to handle the
   results returned from the recognition intent. At the bottom of the class,
   add the following code:

```
@Override
public void onRecognitionDone(int requestCode, String
bestMatch) {
  if (requestCode == VOICE_SETTINGS) {
    boolean result = readPreferences(bestMatch);
    mEditingPreset = bestMatch;
  }
}
```

If the recognition is related to the VOICE_SETTINGS intent code, the `bestMatch`
argument is passed to the `readPreferences` parameter that loads and sets all
temperature bars with preset setpoints. The `mEditingPreset` variable is set so
that we can reuse the preset name during the save process.

We have made all required changes for the `Settings` activity and now can proceed
to use voice recognition in the `Overview` activity to load and set the activated preset.

Using voice recognition to change active presets

Now that users can store different presets, we have to provide a way to change
activated setpoints in the `Overview` activity. Previously, we added a `TextView` class
showing the name of the current preset; to keep the interface lean, we could use
this component also to start voice recognition. The user can change the active preset
through the current flow:

1. When users click on the **TextView** option, the system should start voice
   recognition to get the preset name.

2. If the preset is found, the activated preset should be replaced with the one
   chosen by the user and the `Overview` temperature bars should be updated.

3. If the preset is not found, nothing should happen.

To achieve the preceding interaction flow, proceed with the following steps:

1. As we did for the `Settings` activity, extend the `RecognizerActivity` class from the `Overview` class, in line with the following snippet:

```
public class Overview extends RecognizerActivity implements
OnDataChangeListener {
    //...
}
```

2. Declare the intent request code that we will use to identify and handle the recognized result. At the top of the class, add the highlighted code:

```
public class Overview extends RecognizerActivity implements
OnDataChangeListener {
    public static final int VOICE_PRESET = 1000;
    private AdkManager mAdkManager;
    //...
}
```

3. At the bottom of the class, add a method to start the preset name recognition:

```
public void changePreset(View v) {
    startRecognition("Choose the current preset",
    VOICE_PRESET);
}
```

4. Implement the `onRecognitionDone()` callback to handle the results returned from the recognition intent. Within this method, we call the `setPreset()` member function to update the active preset and load temperature setpoints, if the given preset is found. At the bottom of the class, add the following code:

```
@Override
public void onRecognitionDone(int requestCode, String bestMatch) {
    if (requestCode == VOICE_PRESET) {
        setPreset(bestMatch);
    }
}
```

5. Implement the `setPreset()` method to handle the best recognized result. At the bottom of the class, add the following code:

```
private void setPreset(String name) {
    ArrayList<Integer> values = Preset.get(this, name);
    if (values.size() > 0) {
        Preset.setCurrent(this, name);
        readPreferences();
    }
}
```

6. Connect the `changePreset()` method that starts voice recognition with the `TextView` component. In the `activity_overview.xml` file under `res/layout/`, make the `current_preset` view clickable with the highlighted code:

```
<TextView
    android:id="@+id/current_preset"
    android:clickable="true"
    android:onClick="changePreset"
    android:text="NO PRESET ACTIVATED"
    android:gravity="center"
    android:textColor="@color/coral_red"
    android:textSize="@dimen/text_title"
    android:layout_width="0dp"
    android:layout_weight="2"
    android:layout_height="match_parent" />
```

With this last section, we have created an abstraction to handle voice recognition through Android intents and we have updated the `Settings` and the `Overview` activities to use it. Now we can upload the Chronotherm application and start using the application again with presets and voice recognition features.

Improving user interaction with voice synthesis

Even if the Chronotherm application is working correctly, we have at least one more thing to do: providing proper feedback to let users know the action that was taken. Indeed, both activities fail to provide any visual feedback about what the recognized input is; for this reason, we decided to introduce the voice synthesis API within the initial design.

Because we want to share the synthesis procedure across different activities, we could create a manager that abstracts the synthesis API with a common initialization. The idea is to provide a class that exposes the method to start voice recognition with the given string; we implement it in the following steps:

1. Create the `VoiceManager` class inside the `voice` package.

2. Initialize the class with the following code:

```
public class VoiceManager implements TextToSpeech.OnInitListener {
    private TextToSpeech mTts;
    //...
}
```

This class implements the `OnInitListener` interface that defines the callback that should be invoked after initializing the `TextToSpeech` engine. We store the current `TextToSpeech` instance that we will use in the following snippets as a variable.

3. Override the `onInit()` method so that it sets the US locale if the `TextToSpeech` instance service initialization is successful:

```
@Override
public void onInit(int status) {
  if (status == TextToSpeech.SUCCESS) {
    mTts.setLanguage(Locale.US);
  }
}
```

4. Add the class constructor in which we should initialize the text-to-speech service with the given activity `Context`. Inside the class, write the following code:

```
public VoiceManager(Context ctx) {
  mTts = new TextToSpeech(ctx, this);
}
```

5. Implement the `speak()` method that proxies the given text to the `TextToSpeech` instance, by adding the following code at the bottom of the class:

```
public void speak(String textToSay) {
  mTts.speak(textToSay, TextToSpeech.QUEUE_ADD, null);
}
```

The `TextToSpeech.speak` method uses a queuing strategy to make this method asynchronous. When it's called, the synthesis request is appended in the queue and, when the service is initialized, it will get processed. The queue mode could be defined as the second parameter of the speak method. We can find more information about the text-to-speech service at

http://developer.android.com/reference/android/speech/tts/TextToSpeech.html

Providing feedback to users

We should now adapt our activities to use the simple abstraction implemented in the preceding class. We begin with the `Overview` activity in which we should initialize the `VoiceManager` instance and use it in the `setPreset()` method to provide proper feedback whether we have found the recognized preset or not. To use the synthesis API in the `Overview` activity, perform the following steps:

1. At the top of the class, add the highlighted code between the declaration of variables:

   ```
   private DataReader mReader;
   private VoiceManager mVoice;
   ```

2. At the bottom of the `onCreate()` callback, initialize the `VoiceManager` instance as shown in the following code snippet:

   ```
   mReader = new DataReader(mAdkManager, this, this);
   mVoice = new VoiceManager(this);
   ```

3. Update the `setPreset()` method with the highlighted code so that it calls the synthesis API to provide feedback during preset activation:

   ```
   private void setPreset(String name) {
     ArrayList<Integer> values = Preset.get(this, name);
     String textToSay;
     if (values.size() > 0) {
       Preset.setCurrent(this, name);
       readPreferences();
       textToSay = "Activated preset " + name;
     }
     else {
       textToSay = "Preset " + name + " not found!";
     }
     mVoice.speak(textToSay);
   }
   ```

The prototype is almost done and we only need to repeat the preceding steps for the `Settings` activity. In this activity, we should initialize the `VoiceManager` parameter and make use of the synthesis API in the `onRecognitionDone()` callback. There we should provide feedback to users about what the recognized preset is and whether it's going to be created or edited according to retrieved setpoints. To use the synthesis API in the `Settings` activity, perform the following steps:

1. At the top of the class, declare the `VoiceManager` variable in line with the highlighted code:

```
private String mEditingPreset;
private VoiceManager mVoice;
```

2. At the bottom of the `onCreate()` callback, initialize the `VoiceManager` instance:

```
mVoice = new VoiceManager(this);
startRecognition("Choose the preset you want to edit",
VOICE_SETTINGS);
```

3. Update the `onRecognitionDone()` callback so that it calls the synthesis API to provide proper feedback:

```
@Override
public void onRecognitionDone(int requestCode, String
bestMatch) {
    if (requestCode == VOICE_SETTINGS) {
        String textToSay;
        boolean result = readPreferences(bestMatch);
        if (result) {
            textToSay = "Editing preset " + bestMatch;
        }
        else {
            textToSay = "Creating preset " + bestMatch;
        }
        mEditingPreset = bestMatch;
        mVoice.speak(textToSay);
    }
}
```

We have completed enhancing our prototype with voice recognition and synthesis. The last, missing task is to upload the application again and check whether everything works as expected. Then we can update the Chronotherm application in the `app/build.gradle` file with a `0.2.0` version.

Summary

In this chapter, we managed to introduce numerous features with little work. We learned how to produce a lean and quick user interface with the help of voice recognition and synthesis.

We started our journey creating a new way to store the user's presets, one that required refactoring for both activities and for `SensorThread` temperature checking. We proceed with the first implementation of voice recognition and, to simplify our work, we created a generic activity class extended from the `Settings` and `Overview` activities. This allowed us to abstract some common behavior, making it easy to call the recognition intent within different parts of our code.

As the last step, we prepared the voice synthesis manager to easily use the Android text-to-speech engine. Indeed, we use this component to provide feedback after the recognition process, when users are changing their settings and the current activated preset.

In the next chapter, we will add network capabilities to the Chronotherm application so that it will be able to retrieve forecast data; using this information, we will make a slightly better algorithm to decide whether to turn our boiler on or off.

8
Adding Network Capabilities

In *Chapter 6*, *Building a Chronotherm for Home Automation*, we explored the definition of home automation and, one step after another, we built a prototype capable of controlling a boiler programmatically according to user preferences. We extended this prototype, providing a preset configuration for storing different temperature schedules and also improving the user interaction through voice recognition and synthesis.

This time, we're enhancing the Chronotherm application with another feature that makes use of network capabilities to collect data from the Internet. The goal of this chapter is to make our prototype capable of reacting to external events that can't be easily caught by connected sensors.

In this chapter, we will cover the following topics:

- Extending the Chronotherm application with network capabilities
- Using web services to collect weather forecast data
- Using collected data to change the Chronotherm behavior

Extending Chronotherm with network capabilities

The Chronotherm application solves a specific problem. It turns on the boiler every time the current temperature is below a configured setpoint for each hour of the day. This logic is sufficient for a traditional Chronotherm but we can improve this behavior so it takes into account the strict relationship between the home temperature and weather conditions. For instance, the internal temperature usually drops faster during cold days; if we incorporate this information in the boiler logic, we can make our prototype smarter.

Moreover, if it's really cold, our boiler may stop working because the water inside it has frozen. This issue can be solved if we implement an antifreeze feature that will start the boiler when the outside temperature drops below a defined value despite the user's preferences. Such features would handle unexpected situations when users are away from the house or overnight.

Unfortunately, it's not so easy to wire an external sensor and it may be too complicated to build and use a wireless thermal sensor. However, given that the external temperature is really important, we have to find a workaround to collect weather condition data. Because the UDOO Chronotherm is in our home and it's likely that it's connected to the Internet, we can get this information from web services that provide forecast data, using this knowledge in our computation. In this way, we can even add a complete overview of the weather conditions, improving the user interface while providing users with useful information.

According to the needs mentioned earlier, we can organize our work in the following steps:

1. Implement a module used to connect our prototype to weather REST APIs.
2. Collect and show weather forecast data at regular intervals.
3. Write the boiler antifreeze logic that will use the preceding data.

Connecting to REST APIs

We start our work by providing an implementation to connect to a RESTful web service. **REpresentational State Transfer** (**REST**) is a simple stateless architecture style usually running over the HTTP protocol. The idea behind REST involves exposing the state of the system as a collection of resources we can manipulate, addressing them by their name or ID. The backend service is responsible for persisting resource data, usually through the use of a database server.

When a client asks for a resource through the HTTP protocol, the application server retrieves the resource from the database server and sends it back to the client using an interchange format such as XML or JSON. Exposing a REST API makes it extremely easy to provide data to a mobile client, a browser extension, or any piece of software that needs to access and process application data.

In this chapter, we will use a REST API only for information retrieval. If you are interested in more detail about the REST architecture, follow this link `http://en.wikipedia.org/wiki/Representational_state_transfer`.

Before we begin the implementation of the APIs connector, we should add the following permission (in order to use the Internet in our application) to the `AndroidManifest.xml` file just before the `<application>` tag,:

```
<uses-permission android:name="android.permission.INTERNET" />
```

Then, to provide network capabilities to our application, we have to create an abstraction to the `HttpURLConnection` class so that we can use external services through a simpler API. To create a connector for our application, perform the following steps:

1. Create the `UrlConnector` class in a new package named `http`.

2. At the top of the class, add the following declaration to store the `HttpURLConnection` class instance:

   ```
   private HttpURLConnection mConnector;
   ```

3. Add the following constructor that we will use to initialize the request parameters:

   ```
   public UrlConnector(String encodedUrl) throws IOException {
       URL url = new URL(encodedUrl);
       mConnector = (HttpURLConnection) url.openConnection();
       mConnector.setReadTimeout(10000);
       mConnector.setConnectTimeout(15000);
   }
   ```

   We expect an `encodedUrl` parameter as the argument and we use it to initialize the URL object used later to open the connection. Then we set timeouts for the reading and connection phases, using values that are good for our prototype.

4. Add a generic method to set the HTTP headers of our requests:

   ```
   public void addHeader(String header, String content) {
       mConnector.setRequestProperty(header, content);
   }
   ```

5. Add the following code snippet below the `get()` method that is used to make the call:

   ```
   public int get() throws IOException {
       mConnector.setRequestMethod("GET");
       return mConnector.getResponseCode();
   }
   ```

To the `mConnector` instance, we set the `GET` request method returning the status code of the response. This status code will be used to check whether the request finishes with a success or a failure.

6. Add the following `getResponse()` method to get the result from the web server connection:

```
public String getResponse() throws IOException {
  BufferedReader readerBuffer = new BufferedReader(new
  InputStreamReader(mConnector.getInputStream()));
  StringBuilder response = new StringBuilder();
  String line;
  while ((line = readerBuffer.readLine()) != null) {
    response.append(line);
  }
  return response.toString();
}
```

We create a buffered reader using the `mConnector` instance's input stream and then, through the above reader, we get the content sent by the server. When we've finished, we return the string without any further modifications.

7. Create a `disconnect()` method to close the connection with the server:

```
public void disconnect() {
  mConnector.disconnect();
}
```

The `UrlConnector` class simplifies HTTP calls and this implementation is enough to connect to many web services that don't use any authentication flows. Before we can proceed, we have to choose a web service that provides weather forecast data that we're going to query. For the purpose of our prototype, we will use the OpenWeatherMap service because it provides a free tier without authentication flows, and it's also available through REST APIs. You can find more information at `http://openweathermap.org/` or `http://openweathermap.org/current` for the description of the service and to learn how their REST APIs are structured:

When we make a call to the above RESTful service, we should parse the JSON response, making it available within our application. This approach can be realized with a Java class that knows the response structure and parses it according to our needs. The implementation requires the following steps:

1. Create the `Weather` class in a new package called `weather`.

2. At the top of the class, add the following declarations:

```
private String mStatus;
private double mTemperature;
private int mHumidity;
```

We declare variables according to what we will use from the given response. In our case, we use an `mStatus` variable to store the weather condition so users will know if it's, for example, sunny or cloudy. We also use the `mTemperature` variable, which is our first requirement, and the `mHumidity` attribute to provide a plus to our users.

3. Add the class constructor as follows:

```
public Weather(JSONObject apiResults) throws JSONException,
NullPointerException {
  mStatus = apiResults.getJSONArray("weather").
  getJSONObject(0).getString("description");
  mTemperature = convertTempKtoC(apiResults.
  getJSONObject("main").getDouble("temp"));
  mHumidity = apiResults.getJSONObject("main").
  getInt("humidity");
}
```

We expect as argument a `JSONObject` parameter, the API result after a successful call. From this object, we get the first element of the `weather` field and, within the `JSONObject` object, we get the value of the `description` key. Then we get the `temperature` variable value from the `main` field; this should be passed to a `convertTempKtoC()` function because the returned value from the service is in Kelvin. The last step is to get the `humidity` parameter from the same field. This code could raise some exceptions during JSON parsing and, because of this, we add these exceptions if the constructor throws a list.

4. Add the `convertTempKtoC()` member function, used in the constructor, that converts Kelvin to Celsius:

```
private double convertTempKtoC(double temperature) {
  return temperature - 273.15;
}
```

 This is just an example; you can use any unit of measurement that you prefer for temperature.

5. Add the following getters to the Weather class, to retrieve instance data:

```
public String getStatus() {
  return mStatus;
}

public double getTemperature() {
  return mTemperature;
```

```
    }

    public int getHumidity() {
      return mHumidity;
    }
```

Now that we have an abstraction to make HTTP calls and a JSON results parser, we need to implement the latest building block that calls the REST API and returns a `Weather` instance. We can achieve this implementation through the following steps:

1. Create the `WeatherApi` class within the `weather` package.

2. At the top of the class, declare the following variables:

```
private static final String BASE_URL =
"http://api.openweathermap.org/data/2.5/weather";
private static final String API_PARAM = "?q=%s&lang=%s";
```

The `BASE_URL` attribute defines the endpoint we should call to get weather data. The `API_PARAM` attribute defines the used query string where the `q` parameter is the location we want to query, while the `lang` parameter asks the server to translate the result for the given locale.

3. Define a `static` method to generate a valid request URL:

```
private static String getUrl(String location) {
  String params = String.format(API_PARAM, location,
  Locale.US);
  return BASE_URL + params;
}
```

This method expects a `location` argument used with a valid location to generate the `params` string. In this way, it sets both the `q` and `lang` parameters and then returns the `BASE_URL` attribute with the appropriate concatenation.

4. Add the static method to make the API call and to return an instance of the `Weather` class:

```
public static Weather getForecast(String location) {
  JSONObject results = null;
  Weather weather = null;
  UrlConnector api;
  try {
    api = new UrlConnector(getUrl(location));
    api.addHeader("Content-Type", "application/json");
    // Do GET and grab tweets into a JSONArray
    int statusCode = api.get();
    if (statusCode == HttpURLConnection.HTTP_OK) {
```

```
        results = new JSONObject(api.getResponse());
        weather = new Weather(results);
    }
    else {
      // manage 30x, 40x, and 50x status codes
    }
    api.disconnect();
  }
  catch (IOException e) {
    // manage network errors
  }
  catch (JSONException e) {
    // manage response parsing errors
  }
  return weather;
}
```

This method expects the location argument, which is passed to the getUrl() method we saw earlier to generate the endpoint that should be queried. Through the addHeader() method, we define the request media type as an application/json parameter, used by the server to deduce the format of our request. We make the HTTP call with the api instance correctly configured for our endpoint, checking the status code for a success. After the call, we close the connection, returning the initialized Weather instance or the null reference if an exception is raised.

In this section, we're handling a different status code, an IOException exception, and a JSONException exception that are respectively raised when the API call doesn't finish with a success, when a network error occurs, or when our API call results in a response parsing error. Every time you deal with exceptions in your prototypes, remember that *errors should never pass silently*. We should always handle such errors, notifying the problem to users with proper feedback.

Extending the Android user interface

Now that we can collect weather forecast data through the WeatherApi class, we should start thinking about user interaction. As a first step, we should ask users their home location, updating the Chronotherm user interface with the current selected location and related weather conditions. Second, we should provide a component to set an antifreeze setpoint that can be enabled or disabled, according to the user's preferences.

To achieve both interactions, we can use a clickable `TextView` object that starts voice recognition based on user input, as we did in *Chapter 7, Using Android APIs for Human Interactions*. All the required components are summarized in the following mock-up:

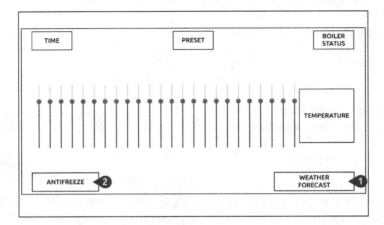

The first step is to update the `Overview` parameter layout. Following the preceding suggestion, we should:

- Add the *Weather Forecast* `TextView`: This component changes whenever a short-lived thread loads a `Weather` instance using the `WeatherApi` class. In this case, it shows the current location, the weather condition, the temperature, and the humidity. When users click on this component, we should launch the voice recognition intent to get the user's location.

- Add the *Antifreeze* `TextView`: This component shows the current antifreeze setpoint with a green color when the antifreeze feature is enabled; on the other hand, it becomes gray when users disable the antifreeze check. When users click on this component, we should launch the voice recognition intent to get the user's antifreeze setpoint; if antifreeze is enabled, the setpoint should be removed from the user's preferences.

We begin working with the layout that can be achieved, updating the `activity_overview.xml` file under `res/layout/` and the `Overview` class, as you can see in the following steps:

1. Change the `LinearLayout` that contains the `view_container` and `temperature` views, with the following highlighted code:

```
<LinearLayout
    android:orientation="horizontal"
    android:gravity="center"
```

```
    android:layout_width="match_parent"
    android:layout_height="0dp"
    android:layout_weight="1">
```

2. Below the previous `LinearLayout`, add the following layout that will containing both TextViews:

```
<LinearLayout
    android:orientation="horizontal"
    android:layout_width="match_parent"
    android:layout_height="0dp"
    android:layout_weight="0.2">
</LinearLayout>
```

3. In the previous container, add the *Antifreeze* and the *Weather Forecast* TextViews with the following code:

```
<TextView
    android:id="@+id/weather_antifreeze"
    android:clickable="true"
    android:onClick="changeAntifreeze"
    android:text="ANTIFREEZE: OFF"
    android:textColor="@color/mine_shaft"
    android:textSize="@dimen/text_title"
    android:layout_width="wrap_content"
    android:layout_height="match_parent"/>

<TextView
    android:id="@+id/weather_status"
    android:clickable="true"
    android:onClick="changeLocation"
    android:text="NO LOCATION SET"
    android:textSize="@dimen/text_title"
    android:gravity="end"
    android:layout_height="match_parent"
    android:layout_width="0dp"
    android:layout_weight="1"/>
```

In both components we define the `onClick` attribute that calls the `changeAntifreeze` and the `changeLocation` methods. These member functions realize the interaction described earlier and we will proceed with their implementation in the next section.

4. Now we should proceed with the `Overview` activity, implementing the missing code to update both TextViews. As the first step, declare their references at the top of the `Overview` class:

```
private TextView mCurrentPreset;
private TextView mTemperature;
private TextView mStatus;
private TextView mWeatherStatus;
private TextView mAntifreeze;
```

5. In the `onCreate()` activity method, get both references with the highlighted code:

```
setContentView(R.layout.activity_overview);
mCurrentPreset = (TextView) findViewById(R.id.current_preset);
mTemperature = (TextView) findViewById(R.id.temperature);
mStatus = (TextView) findViewById(R.id.boiler_status);
mWeatherStatus = (TextView) findViewById(R.id.weather_status);
mAntifreeze = (TextView) findViewById(R.id.weather_antifreeze);
```

6. Because a short-lived thread should update the `mWeatherStatus` TextView parameter, we have to provide a callback in the `OnDataChangeListener` parameter interface that expects a `Weather` instance. Add the highlighted method in the `OnDataChangeListener` parameter interface:

```
public interface OnDataChangeListener {
  void onTemperatureChanged(float temperature);
  void onBoilerChanged(boolean status);
  void onWeatherChanged(Weather weather);
}
```

7. As the last step, add the `onWeatherChanged()` interface implementation with the following code at the bottom of the `Overview` class:

```
@Override
public void onWeatherChanged(Weather weather) {
  if (weather != null && weather.getStatus() != null) {
    String status = "%s: %s, %.1f° (%d%%)";
    status = String.format(status,
      Preset.getLocation(this).toUpperCase(),
      weather.getStatus().toUpperCase(),
      weather.getTemperature(),
      weather.getHumidity()
    );
    mWeatherStatus.setText(status);
  }
```

```
else {
    mWeatherStatus.setText("NO LOCATION SET");
    }
}
```

As we discussed earlier, if we have a `weather` instance we update the `mWeatherStatus` attribute with a formatted string showing the current location, the weather conditions, the temperature, and the humidity.

With the preceding changes, we can upload our Chronotherm application. It presents itself as shown in the following screenshot:

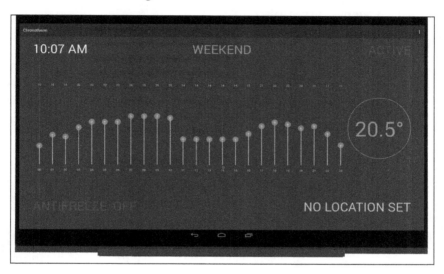

Collecting weather forecast data

Now that our application's user interface is completed, we can proceed to implement the logic to store the user's location while fetching weather data from the RESTful web service. This implementation could be organized in the following steps:

1. Update the `Preset` class to store the user's location.
2. Handle voice recognition results when the user clicks on the `weather_status TextView` parameter.
3. Add a new scheduled thread that fetches weather data and updates the user interface using the `onWeatherChanged()` callback.

We start updating the `Preset` class and realizing it with the following steps:

1. Add, at the top of the class, the highlighted declaration used as a key to store and retrieve the location set by users:

```
private static final String CURRENT_PRESET = "__CURRENT__";
private static final String CURRENT_LOCATION = "__LOCATION__";
```

2. At the bottom of the class, add the following setter to store the given location:

```
public static void setLocation(Context ctx, String name) {
    SharedPreferences sharedPref =
    ctx.getSharedPreferences(SHARED_PREF,
    Context.MODE_PRIVATE);
    SharedPreferences.Editor editor = sharedPref.edit();
    editor.putString(CURRENT_LOCATION, name);
    editor.apply();
}
```

3. To retrieve the stored value, add the following getter:

```
public static String getLocation(Context ctx) {
    String location;
    SharedPreferences sharedPref =
    ctx.getSharedPreferences(SHARED_PREF,
    Context.MODE_PRIVATE);
    location = sharedPref.getString(CURRENT_LOCATION, null);
    return location;
}
```

    Through the CURRENT_LOCATION key, we retrieve the stored location and, if it isn't set, we return a `null` value. In this way, we cover the first run when no location is set, preventing any useless API call.

Now we can proceed with updating the application's interaction to change the currently stored location through voice recognition. To complete this step, proceed with the following changes:

1. At the top of the `Overview` class, add the highlighted declaration to define a request code for the new `Intent` result that will ask for the user's location:

```
public static final int VOICE_PRESET = 1000;
public static final int VOICE_LOCATION = 1002;
```

2. Implement the `changeLocation()` method used by the `weather_status` clickable view:

```
public void changeLocation(View v) {
  startRecognition("Provide your location",
  VOICE_LOCATION);
}
```

3. Implement the member function that will set the current location using the `Preset` class, while providing the appropriate feedback to users:

```
private void setLocation(String location) {
  Preset.setLocation(this, location);
  mWeatherStatus.setText(location.toUpperCase() + ":
  WAITING DATA");
  mVoice.speak("Loading forecast data for " + location);
}
```

After we store the current location in the application's shared preferences, we update the `weather_status` view with a placeholder message until the scheduled thread retrieves the weather conditions.

4. Add the highlighted code into the `onRecognitionDone()` callback, to pass the `bestMatch` parameter to the previous method:

```
if (requestCode == VOICE_PRESET) {
  setPreset(bestMatch);
}
else if (requestCode == VOICE_LOCATION) {
  setLocation(bestMatch);
}
```

The last building block we're missing is to collect and show weather forecast data at regular intervals through a new scheduled thread. This last part can be realized by updating the `DataReader` class with the following steps:

1. At the top of the class, add the highlighted declarations:

```
private final static int TEMPERATURE_POLLING = 1000;
private final static int WEATHER_POLLING = 5000;
private final static int TEMPERATURE_UPDATED = 0;
private final static int BOILER_UPDATED = 1;
private final static int WEATHER_UPDATED = 2;
private AdkManager mAdkManager;
private Context mContext;
private OnDataChangeListener mCaller;
private ScheduledExecutorService mSchedulerSensor;
private ScheduledExecutorService mSchedulerWeather;
```

```
private Handler mMainLoop;
private boolean mBoilerStatus = false;
private Weather mWeather = null;
```

> In the preceding snippet, we set the weather thread polling time to 5 seconds but we have to bear in mind that the external temperature will never change so fast, so it's useless to create too many queries to the web service. We chose this value only for testing purposes; when the prototype is ready, we will need to set more reasonable timings.

2. At the bottom of the class, add the following `Runnable` implementation that collects weather data and publishes the `Weather` instance to the main thread:

```
private class WeatherThread implements Runnable {
  @Override
  public void run() {
    String location = Preset.getLocation(mContext);
    if (location != null) {
      mWeather = WeatherApi.getForecast(location);
      Message message = mMainLoop.obtainMessage
      (WEATHER_UPDATED, mWeather);
      message.sendToTarget();
    }
  }
}
```

3. Add, the new scheduler initialization that spawns short-lived threads for weather data fetching to the `start()` method, as you can see in the highlighted code:

```
public void start() {
  // Start thread that listens to ADK
  SensorThread sensor = new SensorThread();
  mSchedulerSensor = Executors.
  newSingleThreadScheduledExecutor();
  mSchedulerSensor.scheduleAtFixedRate(sensor, 0,
  TEMPERATURE_POLLING, TimeUnit.MILLISECONDS);
  // Start thread that updates weather forecast
  WeatherThread weather = new WeatherThread();
  mSchedulerWeather = Executors.
  newSingleThreadScheduledExecutor();
  mSchedulerWeather.scheduleAtFixedRate(weather, 0,
  WEATHER_POLLING, TimeUnit.MILLISECONDS);
}
```

4. Stop the preceding scheduler, changing the `stop()` method with the following code:

```
public void stop() {
  mSchedulerSensor.shutdown();
  mSchedulerWeather.shutdown();
}
```

5. Update the main thread handler, passing the `Weather` instance to the appropriate callback according to the message type:

```
case BOILER_UPDATED:
  mCaller.onBoilerChanged((boolean) message.obj);
  break;
case WEATHER_UPDATED:
  mCaller.onWeatherChanged((Weather) message.obj);
  break;
```

Now that we have a prototype capable of collecting and showing weather data at regular intervals, we can upload our application into the UDOO board. After we click on the weather status view and insert our location through voice recognition, the application should update the `Overview` interface with the current weather conditions. The next step is to improve the boiler ignition check, adding the antifreeze feature.

Improving the boiler with an antifreeze check

Now that the forecast fetching is up and running, we can proceed with implementing the antifreeze feature. To achieve the interaction and the logic previously discussed, we should:

1. Enhance the `Preset` class storing the user's antifreeze setpoint. In this class, we should provide two utilities to disable the antifreeze check and to find out whether the feature is enabled or not.

2. Handle the antifreeze feature in the `Overview` activity, updating the user interface when a setpoint is selected.

3. Update the boiler logic in the `SensorThread` class so it takes into account the antifreeze check when it's enabled.

We begin our work by changing the `Preset` class with the following steps:

1. At the top of the class, add the highlighted declarations:

```
private static final String CURRENT_LOCATION =
"__LOCATION__";
private static final String CURRENT_ANTIFREEZE =
"__ANTIFREEZE__";
private static final float ANTIFREEZE_DISABLED = -
Float.MAX_VALUE
```

We use the `ANTIFREEZE_DISABLED` attribute as a default temperature that is impossible to reach. In this way, we can match this variable to know whether the antifreeze is activated or not.

2. Add the following setter to store the antifreeze setpoint at the bottom of the class:

```
public static void setAntifreeze(Context ctx, float
temperature) {
    SharedPreferences sharedPref =
    ctx.getSharedPreferences(SHARED_PREF,
    Context.MODE_PRIVATE);
    SharedPreferences.Editor editor = sharedPref.edit();
    editor.putFloat(CURRENT_ANTIFREEZE, temperature);
    editor.apply();
}
```

3. In line with the preceding method, add the following getter to retrieve the antifreeze setpoint:

```
public static float getAntifreeze(Context ctx) {
    float temperature;
    SharedPreferences sharedPref =
    ctx.getSharedPreferences(SHARED_PREF,
    Context.MODE_PRIVATE);
    temperature = sharedPref.getFloat(CURRENT_ANTIFREEZE,
    ANTIFREEZE_DISABLED);
    return temperature;
}
```

With this approach, we return the value of the `CURRENT_ANTIFREEZE` key or the `ANTIFREEZE_DISABLED` attribute, if it isn't set.

4. Add the following method to remove the antifreeze setpoint:

```
public static void disableAntifreeze(Context ctx) {
    SharedPreferences sharedPref =
    ctx.getSharedPreferences(SHARED_PREF,
    Context.MODE_PRIVATE);
```

```
    SharedPreferences.Editor editor = sharedPref.edit();
    editor.remove(CURRENT_ANTIFREEZE);
    editor.apply();
}
```

5. Add the following utility that returns values if the antifreeze feature is enabled:

```
public static boolean antifreezeIsEnabled(Context ctx) {
    return getAntifreeze(ctx) != ANTIFREEZE_DISABLED;
}
```

For the next step, we should add the antifreeze feature in the Overview activity, providing all methods to update the user interface while handling user input through voice recognition. The implementation requires the following steps:

1. At the top of the Overview class, add the mFreeze Boolean that points out whether the antifreeze check is currently activated :

```
private TextView mWeatherStatus;
private TextView mAntifreeze;
private boolean mFreeze = false;
```

2. At the bottom of the class, add the following method used to update the Overview layout:

```
public void updateAntifreeze() {
    float freezeTemperature = Preset.getAntifreeze(this);
    mFreeze = Preset.antifreezeIsEnabled(this);
    if (mFreeze) {
        String status = "ANTIFREEZE: %.1f °C";
        status = String.format(status, freezeTemperature);
        mAntifreeze.setText(status);
        mAntifreeze.setTextColor(getResources().
        getColor(R.color.pistachio));
    }
    else {
        mAntifreeze.setText("ANTIFREEZE: OFF");
        mAntifreeze.setTextColor(getResources().
        getColor(R.color.mine_shaft));
    }
}
```

As the first step, we retrieve the antifreeze temperature available in shared preferences, setting the mFreeze Boolean through the antifreezeIsEnabled() method. At this point, if the antifreeze feature is enabled, we show a green message with the given setpoint; otherwise, we show a gray message stating that the feature is disabled.

3. Call the `updateAntifreeze()` method at the bottom of the `readPreferences()` member function, as we can see in the highlighted code:

```
// ...
mCurrentPreset.setText(activatedPreset.toUpperCase());
updateAntifreeze();
}
```

Now that we have a layout that works with the stored antifreeze setpoint, we should provide users with voice recognition and synthesis to activate or deactivate the antifreeze check. To realize this implementation, the following steps are required:

1. At the top of the `Overview` class, add the highlighted `Intent` request code:

```
public static final int VOICE_LOCATION = 1002;
public static final int VOICE_ANTIFREEZE = 1003;
```

2. Add the `changeAntifreeze()` method to enable or disable the feature, when users click on the `weather_antifreeze` view:

```
public void changeAntifreeze(View v) {
  if (mFreeze) {
    Preset.disableFreezeAlarm(this);
    updateAntifreeze();
    mVoice.speak("Antifreeze disabled");
  }
  else {
    startRecognition("Provide antifreeze degrees",
    VOICE_ANTIFREEZE);
  }
}
```

3. Implement the member function to enable and store the antifreeze setpoint:

```
private void enableAntifreeze(float temperature) {
  Preset.setAntifreeze(this, temperature);
  updateAntifreeze();
  mVoice.speak("Antifreeze set to " + temperature + "
  degrees");
}
```

4. Add the highlighted code to the `onRecognitionDone()` callback, passing the `bestMatch` attribute to the previous method:

```
if (requestCode == VOICE_PRESET) {
  setPreset(bestMatch);
}
else if (requestCode == VOICE_LOCATION) {
```

```
      setLocation(bestMatch);
   }
   else if (requestCode == VOICE_ANTIFREEZE) {
     try {
       float temperature = Float.parseFloat(bestMatch);
       enableAntifreeze(temperature);
     }
     catch (NumberFormatException e) {
       mVoice.speak("Unrecognized number, " + bestMatch);
     }
   }
}
```

If the recognition intent is related to the VOICE_ANTIFREEZE request code, we try to parse the bestMatch parameter as a float, passing the value to the enableAntifreeze() method. If float parsing fails, we provide proper feedback through voice synthesis.

The Chronotherm prototype is almost done; the only task left is to improve the boiler logic using the antifreeze feature. In the DataReader class, we should add the following highlighted code in the isBelowSetpoint() method to make the SensorThread class aware of the antifreeze setpoint, as follows:

```
private boolean isBelowSetpoint(float temperature) {
    int currentHour = Calendar.getInstance().
    get(Calendar.HOUR_OF_DAY);
    String currentPreset = Preset.getCurrent(mContext);
    ArrayList<Integer> currentValues = Preset.get(mContext,
    currentPreset);
    float antifreeze = Preset.getAntifreeze(mContext);
    if (mWeather != null && mWeather.getTemperature() < antifreeze) {
      return true;
    }
    if (currentValues.size() > 0) {
      return temperature < currentValues.get(currentHour);
    } else {
      return false;
    }
}
```

With this code, if the outside temperature is less than the stored antifreeze setpoint, the boiler will turn on regardless of the user's preferences. If this condition doesn't happen, the default behavior continues.

The prototype is completed; through weather forecast data, it keeps our house warm and also removes the risk of the boiler breaking down due to freezing temperatures. We can upload the application and then we can set the antifreeze temperature. The following screenshot shows the expected result:

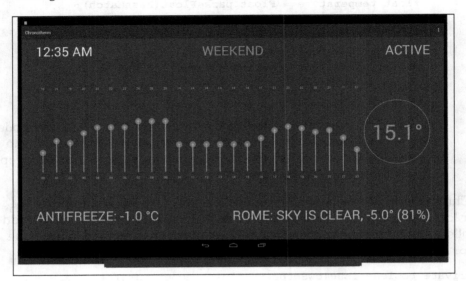

Now that the prototype is completed, we can update the Chronotherm application in the `app/build.gradle` file with a `0.3.0` version.

Summary

In this chapter, we discovered how important the Internet is to our devices, thanks to its huge amount of data and services. We found that our prototype could be improved using the external temperature and, without any changes to the circuit, we collected weather conditions through the network.

In the first part, we wrote a generic connector so we could make HTTP calls without too much work. Then we used this component to implement a partial abstraction of the RESTful web service, capable of retrieving the current weather for the given location. We added new elements in the Chronotherm layout to show forecast data and to handle location input with voice recognition.

Finally, we decided to integrate the external temperature in our boiler logic. Indeed, we implemented antifreeze capability, which turns on the boiler regardless of the user's preferences when the external temperature is too low.

This prototype was this book's last foray into the many features provided by the UDOO board together with the Android operating system. However, if you're interested in one further improvement to the Chronotherm application, you could delve into the bonus chapter, *Chapter 9, Monitoring your Devices with MQTT*, which teaches the main concepts of the *Internet of Things* and the *MQTT protocol*, used to exchange data between physical devices. Even if your next project uses another prototyping board or technology, I hope that you've found useful advice and that you've enjoyed the work we've done together to build simple, but interactive, devices.

Index

Thank you for buying
Getting Started with UDOO

About Packt Publishing

Packt, pronounced 'packed', published its first book, *Mastering phpMyAdmin for Effective MySQL Management*, in April 2004, and subsequently continued to specialize in publishing highly focused books on specific technologies and solutions.

Our books and publications share the experiences of your fellow IT professionals in adapting and customizing today's systems, applications, and frameworks. Our solution-based books give you the knowledge and power to customize the software and technologies you're using to get the job done. Packt books are more specific and less general than the IT books you have seen in the past. Our unique business model allows us to bring you more focused information, giving you more of what you need to know, and less of what you don't.

Packt is a modern yet unique publishing company that focuses on producing quality, cutting-edge books for communities of developers, administrators, and newbies alike. For more information, please visit our website at www.packtpub.com.

About Packt Open Source

In 2010, Packt launched two new brands, Packt Open Source and Packt Enterprise, in order to continue its focus on specialization. This book is part of the Packt Open Source brand, home to books published on software built around open source licenses, and offering information to anybody from advanced developers to budding web designers. The Open Source brand also runs Packt's Open Source Royalty Scheme, by which Packt gives a royalty to each open source project about whose software a book is sold.

Writing for Packt

We welcome all inquiries from people who are interested in authoring. Book proposals should be sent to author@packtpub.com. If your book idea is still at an early stage and you would like to discuss it first before writing a formal book proposal, then please contact us; one of our commissioning editors will get in touch with you.

We're not just looking for published authors; if you have strong technical skills but no writing experience, our experienced editors can help you develop a writing career, or simply get some additional reward for your expertise.

Android Native Development
Kit Cookbook

A step-by-step tutorial with more than 60 concise recipes on
Android NDK development skills

Feipeng Liu

Android Native Development Kit Cookbook

ISBN: 978-1-84969-150-5 Paperback: 346 pages

A step-by-step tutorial with more than 60 concise recipes on Android NDK development skills

1. Build, debug, and profile Android NDK apps.

2. Implement part of Android apps in native C/C++ code.

3. Optimize code performance in assembly with Android NDK.

Android 4: New features for
Application Development

Develop Android applications using the new features of Android
Ice Cream Sandwich

Murat Aydin

Android 4: New Features for Application Development

ISBN: 978-1-84951-952-6 Paperback: 166 pages

Develop Android applications using the new features of Android Ice Cream Sandwich

1. Learn new APIs in Android 4.

2. Get familiar with the best practices in developing Android applications.

3. Step-by-step approach with clearly explained sample codes.

Please check **www.PacktPub.com** for information on our titles

Kali Linux – Assuring Security by Penetration Testing

ISBN: 978-1-84951-948-9   Paperback: 454 pages

Master the art of penetration testing with Kali Linux

1. Learn penetration testing techniques with an in-depth coverage of Kali Linux distribution.

2. Explore the insights and importance of testing your corporate network systems before the hackers strike.

3. Understand the practical spectrum of security tools by their exemplary usage, configuration, and benefits.

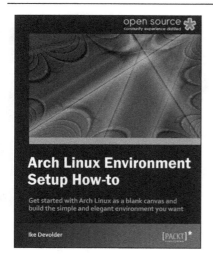

Arch Linux Environment Setup How-to

ISBN: 978-1-84951-972-4   Paperback: 68 pages

Get started with Arch Linux as a blank canvas and build the simple and elegant environment you want

1. Learn something new in an Instant! A short, fast, focused guide delivering immediate results.

2. Install and configure Arch Linux to set up your optimum environment for building applications.

3. Boot and manage services, add and remove packages.

4. Discover and get to grips with the features of the Linux Kernel.

Please check **www.PacktPub.com** for information on our titles